JEAN-YVES BORDIER

# BUTTER
# PASSION

HISTORY, CULTURE, AND RECIPES
FROM BORDIER BUTTER

To my dear parents, Yvette and Jean Bordier,
my beloved wife Réjane,
and our wonderful children, Cécile, Morgane, Jean Marie, Kévin
and their loves!
To our grandchildren "who make us melt like butter!"

Indulge yourselves. Be creative. Be happy for yourselves and your loved ones. Tenderness is no bread-and-butter emotion. Life is a beautiful thing just so long as you understand from the outset that you can't have the butter and the money for the butter!

JEAN-YVES BORDIER

# BUTTER
# PASSION

HISTORY, CULTURE, AND RECIPES
FROM BORDIER BUTTER

PHOTOGRAPHY
Matthieu Cellard

TEXT
Pierrick Jégu
Michel Phélizon
Jean-Yves Bordier

RECIPES
Sylvain Guillemot

ABRAMS | NEW YORK

Vue d'une expédition pour l'Australie
de 4 Barattes-Malaxeurs de 600 litres.

275 ter.

# Preface

"I knew when I started to write this book that it would take me on a fascinating stroll through the museum of my mind – accessing old memories of people and events from the dark recesses of my brain.

Writing your life story is not easy. Memories blur over the years, and the sequence of events becomes confused. You strive for accuracy and economy but there is always a risk that some people or events will slip your mind – doomed to languish forever in obscurity. It's a bit odd revealing yourself to others. It was my wish to entertain my readers and make them curious about my life-long quest to understand everything about butter – about the sociology of butter and the different techniques used to make butter in the course of human history. What started as a simple desire to know more about the practices of my predecessors quickly became an all-consuming passion, and it gave me a particular perspective on the way butter is made today. Take for instance the addition of sea-salt crystals to butter, a business-to-business marketing strategy introduced in the 1990s. Called "fleur de sel", these natural salt crystals helped to redeem butters of indifferent quality (made in a butter-making machine, not a traditional churn) – which could then rightly be promoted as *craquant* or *croquant* (crunchy). The quality of those dairy butters has improved a lot since then.

Here's another insight: you often hear it said today that anything mass-produced is rubbish and everything free-range is good. Now there's an uncompromising attitude! It would be equally unreasonable to claim the opposite. To say this is to misunderstand the history and making of butter, and an unwarranted slight on the high-quality work of French butter producers and their teams in dairies across the country.

Fact is, whether to use raw or pasteurized milk is down to the manufacturer. As a professional producer of artisan butter, I am free to make my own choice, and I'm on the side of that great benefactor of mankind, Louis Pasteur. For me, pasteurization is an integral part of the production process, on a par with working butter on a kneading table. Combining these two processes produces butter with a silky texture and seasonal flavors – an elegant butter that customers seem to love quite as much today as when I first joined the business.

Since 1985 it has been my goal to revive and perpetuate the methods of our ancestors, always working with the rhythms of nature. It was ever my objective to make Bordier Butter a treat for all the senses, "trusted, healthy, honest and truthful," whatever the season.

Respect for our land and respect for our animals. Feeding them well and caring for them well. Looking out for the welfare of the women and men who work in our creameries. For forty-one years now, this has been my life – a full life that's worth telling in these pages."

Jean-Yves Bordier

# CONTENTS

# INTRODUCTION
## MICHEL PHÉLIZON

## The heritage of butter

"Butter is Barbarian fat." This was what the Romans thought back in the early years of our civilization, and the judgement seems doubly perjorative in modern terms. Calling it barbaric denies it refinement. Fat associates it with a body that is out of shape, obesity, diabetes and cardiovascular risks. Pastoral farming (as traditionally practiced by nomadic and semi-nomadic peoples) stood in contrast to arable farming (invented by humans who made the transition to a settled lifestyle). Cain against Abel, Barbarians against civilization, the city against the tribe and, epitomizing the distinction, vegetable oil against butter. Fat itself was not the issue because, in this long-ago period before central heating, the main thing was to keep out the cold. It was a hard life when men and women had to expend considerable muscular energy just to survive. Hence a diet rich in immediately absorbed calories, as provided by the lipides in oil or milk, plus proteins.

Whatever the Romans might have said, butter has been a part of human life for at least 6000 years, since the time when man first domesticated cows, especially for their milk – a crucial food source that was relatively abundant and easy to collect.

Milk is almost a complete food, but it has one major disadvantage. Being unstable by nature, it is highly perishable and spoils quickly. Our ancestors learned by trial and error, and they were quick to grasp two facts: agitate milk, and the fatty particles clump together (forming butter); leave the milk to stand, and it curdles. And when you drain the curd, the proteins clump together (forming cheese). With that, dairy products were born.

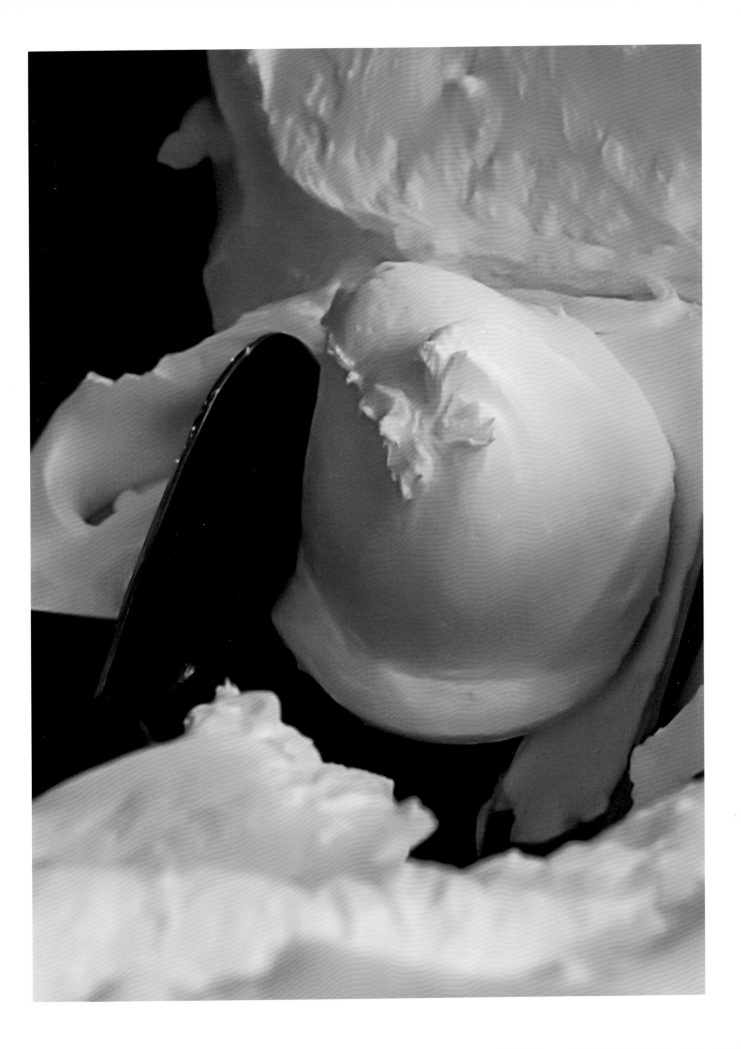

## So what of this "butter, fat of the Barbarians"?

That was the obviously biased and ill-informed opinion of the Romans, the Greeks before them, and probably also the Egyptians. But elsewhere in the Cradle of Civilization, butter was viewed differently – as shown by the famous stone tablets in the Yale Babylonian Collection. Written 1700 years before our time, the tablets are our earliest known culinary reference. They show that the people of this region had mastered the techniques for making and preserving butter in its clarified form, which they used to make highly elaborate dishes, and not just as a basic cooking fat.

It was the same for the Scythians, thirteen centuries before Christ, of whom Montesquieu wrote: "They pierced the eyes of their slaves so that nothing might distract them, and to prevent them from beating their milk." It was true for the Phoenicians, for the people of Carthage, for the Jews and all the people of Northern Europe, especially the Celts who raised vast herds of cattle.

The fact remains however that in olive-growing countries, cows essentially served as working animals and a source of natural fertiliser. Butter, though certainly produced, was used in medicines and cosmetics much more than in cooking, at least by the well-off.

But it would be wrong to assume that butter was a fat reserved for the poor. As Pliny the Elder wrote in his monumental *Natural History* (some 77 years before Christ): "Butter is the choicest food among the barbarian nations, one that distinguishes the wealthy from the common people."

So why this anathematizing of butter as "Barbarian fat"? One explanation is its tendency to go rancid – particularly since the technique for preserving butter by clarification seems to have gradually disappeared in the West, probably replaced by salting. But oil could go rancid too, as pointed out by Pliny the Elder: "Oil unlike wine acquires an unpleasant taste as it ages, and is already old after one year." A particularly illuminating remark when you consider that olives are only harvested once a year! But none of this can have mattered very much to the Romans whose cuisine, as practiced by Apicius and his ilk, relied on bitter, heavily spiced sauces to cover rancid flavors. The same would be true of Medieval cuisine.

Another reason why the Romans disliked butter might have been a simple question of availability. Unlike the arable plains, mountainous regions like the Alps and the Pyrenees offered large areas of natural pasture that favored extensive cattle farming, and thus the production of butter. But other parts of Gaul remained largely forested, which favored pig farming and wild boar. Hence a large reliance on animal fats such as bacon and lard. Vegetable oils from olives and nuts were produced only in a limited geographical area and not widely consumed, being reserved for an aristocratic class fascinated by Roman civilization.

## Butter, peasant food

From the beginning of the 1st century AD, the Gaulish farms of rural France were progressively replaced by larger farms modeled on the "Roman villa". Butter was produced by the Gaulish peasantry for self-consumption and, unlike cheese, was not really a marketable product. Was it therefore reduced to the status of a simple cooking fat? Unlikely, given what we read in Charlemagne's capitulary *De Villis*: "Be sure that bacon and any other dried or salted meats, table wine, mustard, cheese and butter are all made and prepared with the greatest attention to cleanliness."

Four centuries later (c1204) Guiot de Provins writes: "Milk, butter and cheese are greater incitements to licentiousness than animal flesh." The Council of Angers in 1365 then expressly forbad: "Every person of every condition [...] to consume milk and butter in Lent, even with bread and vegetables."

This prohibition lasted for only 126 years, but did paradoxically make butter the preferred cooking ingredient for days of fasting (between 100 and 200 days per year, depending on the diocese). Butter was peasant food, essentially "vulgar", and stayed that way throughout the Middle Ages. It was more or less absent from the first recipe books, though the self-titled Grand Bourgeois de Paris who wrote *Mesnagier de Paris* (1393) did devote a whole paragraph to the de-salting of butter. So there was at least one member of the Parisian upper crust who was aware of butter. He probably spread it on bread and added it to vegetables, treating it as a cooking fat on days of fasting.

# Butter sparks a cooking revolution

Everything changed from the time of the Renaissance, slowly at first, then gathering speed. This interloper butter, which was unknown to Marie de Médicis' Italian cooks, became the marker of a new take on food that is embodied in French cuisine. What happened was a full-blown culinary revolution, driven by the desire to rediscover the real taste of food. The arrival of previously unknown produce from the New World had something to do with it – that and the ability to grow this produce in Europe thanks to advances in farming. There was nothing new about paying close attention to the geographical origins of foodstuffs: the Greeks and the Romans alike took a close interest in the regional distinctions between different varieties of foods. But the revolution that started in the 16th century saw a real will to bring out the flavors of products.

What part did butter play in this? Butter quite simply became the cook's best friend, partly because it is a formidable flavor enhancer (like all fats) and partly because its functional properties served to stimulate creativity. Frying, grilling, browning, sweating vegetables, non-stick cooking, sauce-making, thickening, and not forgetting French patisserie – butter opened up a whole new world of cooking techniques.

# Butter sheds its peasant status

Rising demand gave butter a market beyond the farm, and made it a form of currency for country folk. It captured the attention of the aristocracy who in the second half of the 18th century would create their own model dairies, the most famous being the "hygiene dairy" (*la laiterie de propreté*) in Queen Marie Antoinette's hamlet in the grounds of Versailles. As painters depicted idealized scenes of peasant farming and dairy farming in particular, wealthy consumers became ever more demanding. Consumers in towns now wanted fresh butter with no rancid taste, and even butters with their own distinctive flavors. By the 18th century, certain rare and expensive grands crus of the butter world were much sought after by connoisseurs.

This growing demand for quality and quantity did of course have an impact on supply. Sales networks were established and a new profession sprang up: the butter dealer who bought butters from the farm, blended them together and distributed them to the towns. But there were several obstacles to growth, not least the small size of herds. The "thousand-cow farm" we see today, with Holstein cattle that can produce 10,000 liters of milk per cow (22,000 pounds) for each year's lactation, is a far cry from the typically small farms you saw back then. In 1882, most farms had one cow, three or four at most, each one producing on average just over 1000 liters of milk per year (2,200 pounds), or 3.33 liters per day (7.26 pounds). From that you have to subtract the milk needed to feed the calf, which leaves only a few pounds a day for making butter. Given that it takes just over 21 pounds of milk to make one pound of butter, they would leave the milk to stand for some time, producing acidic creams that, once churned, produced a low-quality butter. To this must be added a variable standard of milking hygiene, and an archaic transport system: the railway only appeared in the second half of the 19th century, refrigeration later still. The contemporaries of 18th century French lawyer and food writer Grimod de La Reynière were forced to admit that most of the butter that found its way to the Paris central market was of poor quality or worse still, downright fraudulent – a situation that got worse in the course of the 19th century.

Great chefs were rightly concerned. With restaurants emerging as positive temples of gastronomy, and bourgeois cuisine making its appearance, demand for butter soared and so, of course, did prices. But while farmers throughout France made butter for private consumption, there was no butter available to the urban masses, even though it was increasingly viewed as a basic necessity. It was at this point that Napoleon III stepped in and launched a competition to find a cheaper substitute for butter: "A butter for the navy and the needy classes, that is cheaper than regular butter and can be kept for a long time without developing that bitter taste and strong smell that so quickly spoils the real thing."

# Butter becomes a mass-produced product

Replace butter with "immitation butter"? Everyone expected this at the beginning of the 1870s. But the idea came to nothing, for several reasons. One was the professionalization of animal husbandry and farm butter production, thanks especially to the first dairy schools. Other factors were the creation of man-made grazing areas, more attention paid to the health of the animals, livestock selection (based on breeding records supplied by the first herd books), the building of cow herds whose yield per animal increased in a spectacular fashion, and the birth of an industry that could handle great quantities of milk. Two major inventions revolutionized the processing of milk: centrifugal separators; and pasteurization, first for milk then cream. The first certainly made it possible to process great quantities of milk, and it was also economical enough to allow small-scale farm production to continue, especially in the west of France. The second invention, in addition to its significant impact on hygiene, had the important advantage of extending the shelf life of fresh butter (but the disadvantage of being only available to dairies.) Then there were the many improvements in churns and the kneading of butter, thanks chiefly to the invention of the *malaxeur rotatif plateau avec sa vis cannelée* (rotary kneading table). This tool was quickly adopted by the butter traders to produce a better quality (albeit increasingly standardized) product by mixing farm-made butters from different sources. The growing availability of cold storage, both industrial and in domestic refrigerators, also played a major role in the "democratization of butter". Butter gradually became affordable for all, with per-capita consumption doubling between 1958 and 1988. On the one hand, cooking with butter was still a key feature of French gastronomy. On the other hand, the industrialization of butter production thanks to mechanization and the widespread use of continuous butter-making machines, led to a product uniformity that product branding could not conceal. Butter had lost its original aromas. It had become impoverished.

# Bordier Butter: so much more than a fat

Butter was back to being a basic fat, not the fat of the Babarians twenty centuries earlier, but a product for mass consumption. According to nutritionists indeed, butter belongs in the same category of fats as oil and margarine. It is not a milk product in its own right, unlike liquid milk, cheese, yoghurt, milk-based desserts and the other fresh milk products that have hit supermarket shelves. Some bucked the trend, and that was the great strength of Jean-Yves Bordier. This is a butter craftsman who focuses on the source of his raw material: milk, as produced by responsible, small-scale dairy farmers whose cows graze on grass from spring to autumn. His savoir faire and production techniques date from the close of the 19th century, but his patience is all his own. Jean-Yves Bordier allows his butter time to develop its bouquet, prefers manual to machine processes, and has all the savvy required to supply the tables of great starred restaurants with "couture" butters.

Bordier Butter is not a "fat". It is a prized ingredient in great cuisine, and also a foodstuff in its own right. Jean-Yves Bordier is not so much an inventor as a re-discoverer of butter. A man who saw a way to adapt a unique and ancestral product and make it fit our modern lifestyles, without sacrificing its soul.

Being passionate about the flavors in butter, it is no surprise that he has sought to combine these flavors with others, so creating flavored butter blends. These too are inspired by the culinary tradition of France, inviting you to explore new tastes and new sensual delights.

# THE WORD
# "BUTTER"

The word "butter" (*beurre*) started as a spoken word that was eventually written down. That's what makes it such a vigorous word – a reflection, if you like, of everyday living. The word as we use it today is the result of more than two thousand years of semantic evolution.

In 1982 the French historian and Assyriologist Jean Bottéro translated three cuneiform tablets from the Yale Babylonian Collection: three small clay slabs, dating from about 1700 BC, recording life in Mesopotamia. He followed up with a book, *La Plus Vieille Cuisine du Monde* (The Oldest Cuisine in the World), which looks at the preoccupation with the gastronomic arts in Babylonian culture, and the way food and cooking shape our lives. It provides a wealth of details on the staple foods of the time and how they were processed, and it identifies the first known use of "butter". In the Cradle of Civilization it was called *hymetus*.

Ancient Greek civilization then saw the emergence of another word, *bouturon*, from *bous* (ox, cow) and *turos* (cheese). Hippocrates used it in his medical writings to describe the fat content in milk, which he said lay heavy on the stomach. It seems that Hippocrates, far from being a fan of butter, was more "galactophobic" than "galactophilic" – an aversion he shared with the rest of the Ancient Greeks.

The Ancient Romans likewise looked down on butter. For them it was a fat fit only for the Barbarians who produced it: those consummate butter-eaters the Vikings, who were rebelling against Roman forces in the north of the Empire. The fact that the much-despised early Christians also liked butter did it no favors either. The Romans seem to have used butter, or *butyrum* as it was known by then, as an ointment for the skin and hair. Roman women found it made their skin whiter and left their hair soft and shiny. Eventually the word *butyrum* gave way to *bure* (Old English *butere*), before *beurre* and "butter" took hold in the 15th century.

Elsewhere in the world, the food we know as butter has been indirectly affected by climate. In very hot countries, for example, butter is clarified: heated gently until it melts

to separate the water and milk solids (proteins, lactose) from the butterfat. Clarified butter has a long shelf life, can be stored at room temperature and makes a more practical alternative to ordinary butter. In India they call it *ghee* and produce more of the stuff than any country on Earth (sold in bottles and tins alike). In Egypt they call it *samna* and in Morocco they call it *smen*. The Fulani call it *niter kibbeh* and the northern Brazilians call it *manteiga da garaffa* (butter in a bottle) or *manteiga da terra* (butter of the land).

Another interesting fact you might not know: the word "butter" together with butter itself only appeared in Southeast Asia and Japan 70 years ago, courtesy of globalization, and then only in the upper echelons of society. In France, the word *beurre* became a protected word in 1897 before being officially defined by a law passed in 1905 – a necessary step to protect consumers from spiraling fraud and misrepresentation in relation to the making and selling of butter.

The term "butter" has meanwhile been appropriated by the chemical, pharmaceutical, cosmetics and patisserie industries to describe products with the look and feel of butter. Butter of antimony is mentioned in *L'Encyclopédie de Diderot et d'Alembert* as early as the 17th century! Cocoa butter and Shea butter or *Cupuacu* followed in the 20th century. The term "butter" is now a tool for semantic advertising, just as the terms Sel de Noirmoutier and Guérande are used to promote butters of indifferent quality. It is hard to believe that the same women's magazine can paradoxically sing the praises of so-called Shea "butter" then a few pages later condemn consumption of the real thing – exploit the semantics of butter but lambaste butter itself.

Then there is Zebda: a prime example of those linguistic shifts that make the French language so rich and expressive of our multicultural ideals. Zebda is the Arabic word for *beurre*, and the name chosen by a French music group from Toulouse whose songs are about *beur* culture (which is French slang for Arabs in general and the French-born children of North African parents in particular). It just goes to show how butter is a traditional food on both sides of the Mediterranean – a food and not a social issue, created in a spirit of dialogue and sharing

- I -

# BORDIER BUTTER

## BUTTER WITH A PEDIGREE

# BORDIER
## — *given name* Jean-Yves

How did Jean-Yves Bordier, born in the Val-de-Marne in the Ile-de-France region, wind up in the port of St. Malo in Brittany making one of the most famous butters in France? Thanks to hard work and inspiration of course, but also thanks to breeding, good luck and meeting the right people.

# From Saint-Maur to St. Malo

Our story begins on Friday 28 October 1955 at 1.50 pm in Saint-Maur-des-Fossés in the Paris suburbs. On the Tuesday after his birth, the young Jean-Yves is warmly wrapped up by his mother and placed in a large wooden crate (*canadienne*) containing 1,440 eggs packed in straw to prevent them breaking in transit. Next stop: the market, to sell the eggs but also slabs of salted and unsalted butter kneaded by Jean-Yves' maternal grandparents, the butter-makers Corentine and Corentin Raphalen. In 1919, the couple left the Bigouden region of their native Brittany and headed first for Villedieu-les-Poêles in Normandy, before settling in 1948 in Saint-Maur-des-Fossés to be closer to their Parisian clientele. Jean Bordier, Jean-Yves' father, eventually abandoned butter-making and instead became a *fromager-affineur* (cheesemonger and finisher). Then along came a daughter, baby Catherine. The young Jean-Yves relished his happy childhood, not least the holidays he spent by the sea with his grandmother in Bénodet on the south Finistère coast in western Brittany. His attitude to school was always fairly casual but – remembering those seaside escapades

– he was ready with an answer when his father popped the dreaded question: "What do you want to do?" "Join the merchant navy," came the reply and with that, after graduating from high school, our young Parisian entered the Lycée Kersa in Paimpol – a preparatory school for the French Merchant Marine, run by the De La Salle Christian Brothers. Jean-Yves had always wanted to live by the sea, so he spent most of that preparatory year sailing, not sitting at a school desk. His antics cost him the entrance exam to the French Merchant Marine Academy. Jean Bordier was not amused. Enough was enough, he said. "You've had your fun, time for some work." The wayward son was summoned back to Paris where he found himself doing what he had always done. Turning the cheeses. Washing out the buckets used to contain the cream cheese. Helping his parents unload the truck on its return from the central market and lending a hand on market stalls. Eventually he was ready to follow his father into the profession and learn the serious business of cheese-making and finishing. Mastering ripening techniques and discovering ways to manage a stock of live goods with tastes and textures that changed from day to day.

## THE MOVE
## TO ST. MALO

Jean-Yves' first store opened in 1982, in Lannion northwestern Brittany, and proved a roaring success. Encouraged by the glowing reports he received from food critics, he decided to expand. In 1985, his friend Roger Brionne told him there was a charming dairy for sale in St. Malo. What made this place special was butter-making processes that had not changed since the early 20th century – the same or nearly the same as those practiced by Jean-Yves' butter-maker-and-kneader grandfather. It was a real find. On 28 November 1985, Jean-Yves purchased number 9 Rue de L'Orme – a dairy located in the heart of the ancient walled city of St. Malo. He called it "La Maison du Beurre". It was a turning point, the moment when Jean-Yves' passion for butter really took root. Month after month, our expert cheese crafter learned enough about butter to develop his own manufacturing processes. His ambition was to become a "real" butter artisan – and he went all out to make that happen. He interviewed

"Jean-Yves had always wanted to live by the sea"

old-hands, devoured instruction manuals dating from the turn of the 20th century, and urged his suppliers to be particularly careful about cattle feeding – even if this meant paying a premium for quality. His hard work paid off: the name Bordier is now inseparably linked to butter.

## BORDIER BUTTER STEPS OUT BEYOND THE RAMPARTS

In 1995, Jean-Yves' work in St. Malo attracted the attention of Parisian celebrity chef Eric Briffard. That same year, the equally talented and gracious Alain Passard became one of the first Michelin-starred chefs to welcome Bordier Butter into his Paris restaurant. Thanks to his two famous "promoters", Jean-Yves' reputation spread like wildfire and what started as an insider's secret became public knowledge. Another boost to his business career was the call he received one morning from the late French baker and entrepreneur, Lionel Poilâne. In 1997, Jean-Yves was invited to the Angoulême Comic Strip Festival to take part in a debate on gastronomy and food, alongside fellow panelists Jean-Pierre Raffarin, chefs Marc Veyrat and Yves Camdeborde, and journalist Dominique Lacout, author of the *Livre Noir de la Cuisine*. He suddenly found himself catapulted to the center of the food world stage, and expected to offer an opinion. Bordier Butter was already on the shelves of Lafayette

Gourmet. By 1998 it was selling out fast at the Grande Epicerie gourmet food hall (part of Bon Marché) and delighting the patrons of leading chefs Guy Savoy (the first to request a custom-salted butter), Alain Senderens and Eric Fréchon. Custom-packaged Bordier Butter had meanwhile carved a niche for itself in luxury hotels – boosting a reputation that now reached far beyond the walls of St. Malo, the former home of the corsairs. By 1999 its success was unstoppable, at home and also abroad. Jean-Yves looked for improvements at every point in the production process. He fine-tuned the kneading stage and used different types of paddles depending on the butter, starting with his fabulous seaweed butter. To produce this at all required

real ingenuity – overcoming teething problems without ever resorting to the convenience of modern technology.

## INTERNATIONAL RECOGNITION

The year 1999 marked a milestone in the history of Bordier Butter. As Jean-Yves explains: "It was the year of my unforgettable meeting with the Clanchin family, owners of the Triballat dairy in Noyal-sur-Vilaine, near Rennes – the year when confidence in Bordier Butter's future seemed assured." Whatever his detractors may say, Triballat's acquisition of Bordier had no effect on Jean-Yves' commitment to quality. On the contrary, it gave him the means to

# Following on from seaweed butter, Jean-Yves has given us Yuzu butter, smoked salt butter, butter with Espelette chili and lemon-olive oil butter

pursue his work in ideal conditions. In 2005 the butter workshop and cheese-maturing rooms moved to comfortable and spacious premises built to European standards. With them came the traditional methods dear to Jean-Yves' heart, but carefully incorporated within a modern framework as required by export regulations. Because Bordier Butter is now exported worldwide. "With the opening of the Tokyo point of sale, the Japanese equivalent of our Galeries Lafayette, and demand growing from Denmark and top London restaurants, I realized that Bordier Butter was on its way. We've come far over the past three decades," says Jean-Yves. "That encounter with kneading and boxwood paddles in 1985 was just the beginning." Today he fulfills all the functions of a CEO but remains closely involved with product development. The invention of flavored butters is a case in point: following on from seaweed butter, Jean-Yves has given us Yuzu butter, smoked salt butter, butter with Espelette chili and lemon butter.

And he has plenty more surprises up his sleeve – because what this epic adventure into butter composition is really about is cooking with butter.

## MEDIA ATTENTION

Jean-Yves' work attracted media attention almost from the very beginning – a coverage that intensified through encounters with prominent chefs and influential journalists. There was his meeting with Martine Albertin at the Salon des Saveurs in Paris – a grand dame of food journalism and the author of many recipes based on Bordier Butter, most notably for *Madame Figaro* magazine. Also with François Simon, "one of the first to realize something very important about our products: the softness and complexity that makes them inherently fragile." Over the years, Jean-Yves' work has been faithfully documented by Yvon Le Chevestrier for the regional daily newspaper *Ouest-France*, not to mention journalist Sébastien Lapaque's "clear-eyed" reporting for *Le Figaro*. Late 2002 brought news of two forthcoming nominations, first as *Fromager de l'Année 2003* (cheese-maker

of the year) in the Guide Pudlowski, a distinction conferred on Jean-Yves by his dear departed friend Lionel Poilâne; then a few weeks later, as *Crémier de l'année 2003* (dairyman of the year) in the Guide Champérard. In 2006 Jean-Yves featured on the back page of *Libération* in an article by Marie-Dominique Lelièvre describing his work philosophy and wittily entitled *Saint mi-sel* (a slightly salty saint). The gospel according to Bordier has also aired on radio – on Europe 1, where Jean-Yves was invited by Julie Andrieu, and on RTL at the behest of journalist Virginie Garin. Television programs featuring his handiwork include *Envoyé Spécial* on France 2, *Des Racines et des Ailes* on France 3 and *100 % Mag* on M6, which was then hosted by Estelle Denis. Loïc Ballet once turned up in St. Malo on his famous *triporteur* (butcher's bike) to interview Jean-Yves for *Télematin*. Chef and TV presenter Cyril Lignac meanwhile rode down to Brittany on his motorcycle and sidecar to butter up Jean-Yves for *Le Chef de France*.

# A BUTTER ARTISAN, sailor and gourmet

But Jean-Yves Bordier does not exist for butter alone. In his other life he is a yachtsman, riding the waves all the way to the rocky outcrops of the Chausey archipelago. As a committed member of the Mémoire et Patrimoine des Terre-Neuvas association, he also takes a keen interest in the social history of St. Malo as a major maritime hub. Bordier Butter was being enjoyed off the coast of Terre Neuve (Newfoundland) by the early 1990s – the end of a great period in French maritime history that had begun in the 16th century.

"For me, heading out to sea is as important as breathing. I feel good when I'm sailing, serene you could say. I come from a seafaring family that prides itself on having bred four professional sailors. The sea teaches us humility. Sailing around the Channel Islands, along the Brittany coast, in the Mediterranean or across the Atlantic sharpens your perception of life." The sea is his mistress, as also is literature. "Life would not be possible without books – books and sharing a bottle of wine or a good meal with friends are among the greatest pleasures in life." It is this innate fascination with the culinary world that makes our man such a discerning gourmet. Raised by parents who savored the good things in life, he embraced his destiny as a cheese-monger, finisher and butter-maker then naturally gravitated towards the best people in the business – artisans, producers, bistro owners and chefs of exceptional talent and skill. Junk food has always

been anathema to Jean-Yves, welcome neither at his table nor in his stores. His commitment to good food is obvious from the moment you set foot in La Maison du Beurre in St. Malo – the ham cellar lined with pork meats; the delicious biscuits from the Maison du Pain in St. Malo: the La Quiberonnaise sardines in Bordier Butter; the caramels made with Bordier Butter; and the range of hand-crafted wines from vineyards across France. Jean-Yves is a frequent visitor to natural wine salons. "I had the good fortune to meet Anthony Cointre, no ordinary cook but a travelling chef who taught me about the extraordinary destiny of grapes. He and another chef supremo, Chris, from L'Arsouille Restaurant in Rennes, lined up a wine tasting that just blew me away – moved me and made me happy too. To be happy in the kitchen is to take pleasure in sharing the taste experience – as I do with Loïc Lucas, a chef who has taught me so much!"

# The making

It takes 60-72 hours to make Bordier Butter from the point of milk reception to finished product, depending on the season. That time drops to about six hours for mass-produced butter. The comparison is meaningful because butter, like bread and other traditional products, needs time to develop complexity and richness. Butter factories largely eschew such ambitions and focus instead on making enormous quantities of butter in record time using a continuous butter-making machine. Output from the Bordier butter workshop is "just" 400 tonnes per annum, based on a process that is not continuous, with attention to detail from start to finish. As Jean-Yves points out, 400 tonnes is just enough to meet demand from a growing clientele at home and abroad. It is not enough "as wrongly suggested by one reporter, to exceed demand from top French restaurants. That would take tens of thousands of tonnes, which means tens of thousands of cows since you need 22 liters of milk to produce one kilo of butter and we have nothing like that many ..."

# Good BUTTER requires GOOD MILK

No one knows this better than Jean-Yves, who only sources his milk from top-flight producers in the area between Rennes, the northern end of Ille-et-Vilaine and the southern end of the Manche Department. All of them practice organic farming. Milk is after all no ordinary fluid. Milk is a food, the very first food. Milk conjures up images of motherhood and was a mark of every ancient civilization – Egyptian, Roman, Indian, Sumerian and Nordic alike.

So what makes "good milk"? In addition to specific health criteria that are required by law, milk must possess certain technical, bacteriological and organoleptic characteristics that make for good cream, good butter and good cheese – characteristics linked to the cows and the farmers who care for them.

Good milk these days is also milk that respects the seasons. Cattle feed is a priority here so farmers cannot afford to make mistakes. In spring and summer, cows should graze on small flowers and grass high in chlorophyll and beta-carotene. In fall they should graze on cover crops. In winter and early spring when new shoots appear, they require home-produced forage representing a mix of flowers and grass as decided by the farmer. And talking of grass, "barn-drying obviously makes for better quality hay," says Jean-Yves. Though practiced by too few producers, barn-drying produces hay for winter feeding with much of the nutritional value of fresh pasture. Home produced silage is the alternative to corn silage – often the only forage for dairy cattle even though it does little good to the cows and even less good to the environment.

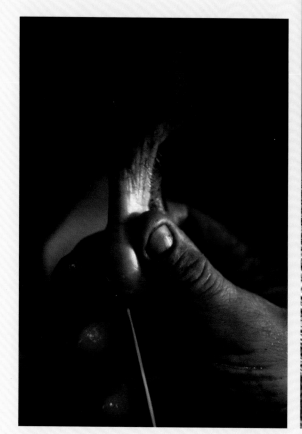

Milk, as the ultimate expression of forage and pasture, conveys the very essence of terroir. To make the finest, most flavorful butter you need the finest milk and that depends on well-fed cows. It's as simple as that. Top-quality milk is a non-negotiable requirement. "I think that non-organic products should be labeled as such – not the other way around. It's absurd that people who do their job properly should be forced to justify themselves and shout it from the rooftops," says Jean Yves. "Going organic means refusing pesticides, nitrites and all the other inputs dear to agribusiness." That also implies accepting that Bordier Butter is a living product, with characteristics that change with the season. It can be pale and brittle in February, then smoother in spring with a silkier texture, richer aromas and an extraordinary buttercup-yellow color. Telling him that his butter changes color with the seasons is the greatest compliment anyone can pay to Jean-Yves Bordier.

# FRENCH DAIRY FARMERS

## PATRICIA AND PHILIPPE MORIN

B ordier Butter is born on the farm not in the butter workshop. No one knows that better than Jean-Yves, which is why he has so much respect for those traditional dairy farmers, committed to organic production, who provide him with first quality milk for his first quality butter. Milk and nothing else is what gives butter its flavor profile – those characteristics that vary with the terroir and the season. Yes, Jean-Yves feels immensely grateful to his friends the farmers and visits them regularly. People like Patricia and Philippe Morin, a husband-and-wife team who work a 60-hectare dairy farm in a little place called Le Rocher Nourri, just outside Montours, at the northern end of the Ille-et-Vilaine department. Their herd comprises 70 milk cows, mostly Holsteins plus a few Jerseys. But then the size of the herd is immaterial. "It's not the size of the farm that matters but what you do with it," says Patricia. Her husband opted to go organic within three years of taking over the reins from his parents in 1995. Patricia then joined him in 2006, having first gone back to school to study agriculture. These are two people who know what they want: to feed mankind

using an ecologically sustainable and animal-friendly approach, producing quality milk thanks to carefully seeded pasture and carefully managed grazing. "More work definitely but as our returns show, well worth it in the end." The couple grow their own forage and employ a barn hay drying system to make sure their cows stay well fed outside the growing season. And how does Triballat fit into all of this? "Triballat buys our organic milk at the right price. It's as simple as that. Plus they're approachable, they listen and I think they rather admire farmers like us," says Patricia. And their relationship with Jean-Yves Bordier? "Let's not call him Bordier, he's just plain Jean-Yves to us. I remember the first time we met. He came with a production manager from Triballat to ask if they could sit in on the milking. We were more than happy to oblige. Not for the money since money was never mentioned, but because of the look in Jean-Yves' eyes – you could see he was honest, generous and passionate about what we did. And how proud we are today to help him make his exceptional butter! I can think of no finer reward and no greater happiness!"

# Patience and dexterity

Practiced hands bring precision and elegance, employing slow, deliberate movements that pay homage to timeless traditions.

## CREAMING ... THEN RIPENING!

Butter-making proper commences once the milk is collected. The first stage is creaming: separating the cream from the milk. This is done by centrifugation using a process invented in 1878 by various engineers then perfected by a Swedish scientist called Gustaf De Laval, whose invention revolutionized the dairy industry. Before that, milk straight from the cow was left for a day or so in large, shallow vessels until the cream rose to the surface (the fat globules being the lightest particles in milk) and could be skimmed off. The Triballat dairy creams its milk fresh from the farm.

Milk collected from the producer in the morning is delivered to the dairy in the late afternoon and creamed that same evening. The cream is then left to ripen for a period of 12-36 hours depending on the season. Before churning, the cream is inoculated with lactic acid bacteria that convert lactose into lactic acid. The resulting cream ranges from sweet to sour, short- to long-lived – it all depends on what the butter-maker has in mind. Known as natural ripening, this stage plays no part in a commercial manufacturing system. It requires time and patience and essentially serves to bring out the cream's complex bouquet, which is showcased by churning.

## CHURNING –
## THE IMPORTANCE
## OF TRADITION

Churning is the process of shaking up cream to make butter, taking its name from the churn that is used for the purpose. Churns first appeared in the 16th century and were originally conically shaped, before acquiring the cylindrical or sometimes square shape that we see today. As churning proceeds, the cream changes from liquid to solid (butter), reversing the more familiar transition from solid to liquid. To put it simply, you start with fresh liquid cream and beat it to make whipped cream. The longer you beat the cream the thicker it becomes and the more it starts to resemble butter. Technically speaking, the ripened cream is heated to 14°C (57.2°F), poured into the churn and agitated for an initial period of 50 minutes. This causes the fat globules to clump together and form butter grains, leaving behind the buttermilk, a mixture of water and protein that is drained off. All that remains in the churn are the butter grains, which must now be washed to remove any residual buttermilk. This involves adding a quantity of iced water

then moving the churn forward and backward until washing is complete. This rinsing water is then likewise drained off and replaced with a volume of iced water equivalent to the quantity of buttermilk removed at the close of the first stage. The difference in temperature between the cream (14°C/57.2°F) and the iced water causes the butter grains to contract and agglomerate as the churn is rotated. Churning is a crucial stage in the making of good butter, yet it accounts for just 0.1 per cent of French production, which naturally includes Bordier Butter. These days, the overwhelming majority of manufacturers use a continuous butter-making machine. "Continuous butter-making is much faster and requires much less manpower, but it dramatically alters the molecular profile of the fat content. Basically, it makes butter viscous and greasy. Which is a far cry from the excellent results you get when high-quality cream is churned properly," says Jean-Yves. He sees the churn as a primary tool in the expression of terroir – the process that unlocks the potential in butter to be what he calls "Nature's blotting paper."

## KNEADING –
## THE BORDIER STROKE
## OF GENIUS

Jean-Yves Bordier does not just make butter. He transforms it. It is his choice to follow the methods of the 19th century, when butter came from a fragmented pattern of localized production. When there was a specialist for every stage of production and everybody pulled together to make butter. Jean-Yves watches over everything, from the quality of the raw materials to the butter-making process itself. But it is at the kneading stage that his experience "makes all the difference." Kneading was originally invented as a means to blend butters from different farms in the hope that the end product would taste good. For Jean-Yves, kneading is what makes his butter sublime. These days most producers knead their butter directly in the churn – the quickest method certainly, but it contradicts the idea of taking the time to do the job properly. Jean-Yves prefers to use a kneading table. He finds this improves the texture of the butter, makes it extraordinarily silky and deliciously "spreadable", while also bringing out powerful and complex aromas that offset the neutralizing effect of pasteurization. Because Bordier Butter is pasteurized butter – to help it last longer and ensure it is safe to eat. "I'm with Louis Pasteur - a great

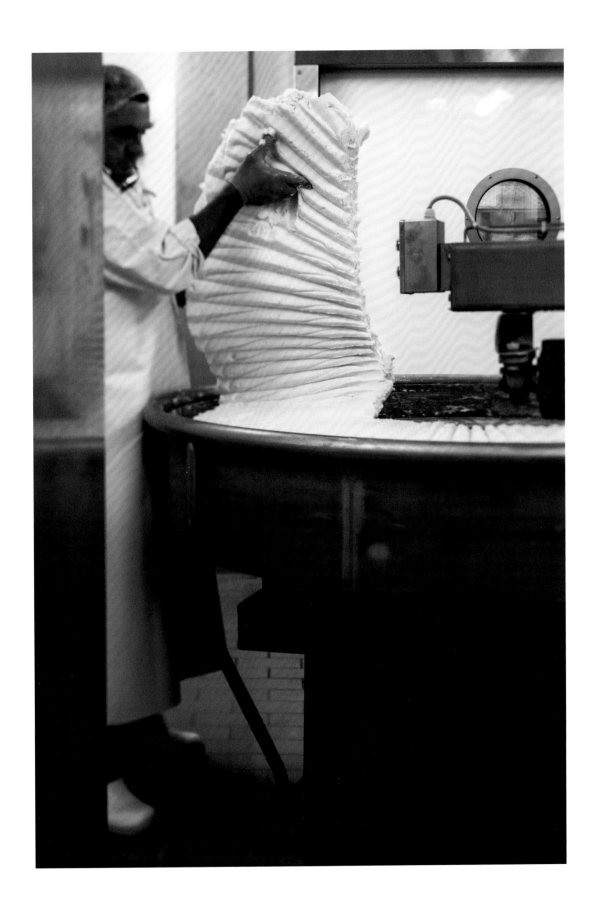

# "When my butter cries it means it is singing ... when it sings it means it is crying"

scientist who invented pasteurization to improve public health. It was certainly not his intention to prevent the manufacture of good food aimed at raw-milk aficionados – which includes myself, except that I'm not stupidly dogmatic about it. Let's not forget that milk straight from the udder is protected by good bacteria that kill off the bad bacteria for the first six hours. But beyond that point non-refrigerated milk can pose a serious health risk if it isn't boiled."

So how is butter kneaded in the Bordier workshop? Picture a circular platform fitted with a wooden roller and a man wrestling valiantly with 50 kilos (110 pounds) of butter. "I spent 28 years kneading before handing over to my colleagues. You have to understand the joy of plunging your hands into a mass of butter, rolling it into a ball at the rate of four turns a minute, being careful not to overwork it, knowing when to stop so that, at the height of summer for instance, you always end up with a lovely texture and enticing scents of caramel," explains Jean-Yves. The effect of the wheel, combined with salting, works the surplus water out of the butter. This concentrates the flavors, which are further intensified through oxidation. One big advantage of the kneading table is that it keeps the butter in contact with the air, unlike the kneading done in the *baratte*. As the wheel gradually squeezes the water out of the butter, you can hear the butter "crackle". Or as Jean-Yves puts it: "When my butter cries it means it is singing ... when it sings it means it is crying."

Kneading is a physical, sensual and exacting process. The kneader must watch and listen carefully, working each mass of butter according to its characteristics, the season and the weather. Kneading times range from about 15 minutes in summer to half an hour in winter. Jean-Yves reckons it takes at least three years to become proficient at kneading, to get a real feel for it. Kneaders, like the farmers who produce the milk and the "little hands" who shape the butter, embody a human dimension that no longer matters in the dairy industry but still matters very much for Jean-Yves Bordier.

## A SPRINKLING
## OF SALT ...

In the course of kneading, fine salt (50 microns) is sprinkled over the butter and worked in. The House of Bordier has never succumbed to the fashion for adding salt crystals to butter, mainly because of the risk of uneven salting but also out of respect for local customs. As Jean-Yves explains: "The people of these parts used to obtain their salt by simply boiling down seawater in large, flat pans then scraping off the salt that was left behind after the water evaporated – a very fine salt with a very small grain." The Bordier salting method produces an important effect on the butter. "The salt I sprinkle over my butter gets crushed by the kneading wheel, causing the fat molecules to react and release their water. That's when you see the butter "cry", referring to those

tear-like drops of water that well up to the surface of all grass-fed and craft-made butter." This is also the point at which the amount of salt is decided, adding salt to suit the requirements of different customers, chefs and styles of cooking – an idea of Jean-Yves' aimed at the bespoke market. After kneading and salting, the butter is shaped by hand then pressed through a butter cutter that divides it up without damaging its molecular structure.

## SHAPING –
## GREAT DEXTERITY AND
## CLOCKWORK PRECISION

Anyone who has ever watched Jean-Yves Bordier or his colleagues "shape butter" with boxwood or metal paddles might think it was purely for show. But however entertaining his customers might find it, the shaping of Bordier Butter is a serious business requiring stamina and precision. Traditionally, until the appearance of the first butter molds in the 18th century, all butter was shaped using spoons, ribbed paddles and wooden

knives. As Jean-Yves explains: "Butter-shaping serves to form our classic bars and at the higher end of production we also use it to create one-off butters for individual customers. So when I hear it said that we are no better than industrial manufacturers, I feel disappointed on behalf of my teammates, and angry at the rank ingratitude displayed by people who should know better – people who were invited to come and see us at work but never showed up."

The attention, care, and clockwork precision that goes into shaping particular orders for particular chefs has to be seen to be believed. Dexterity too, particularly when shaping mini pats of butter weighing just 25-70 grams (0.88-2.4 ounces). It is no mean feat to create bespoke butter portions for the tables of luxury hotels and Michelin-starred restaurants, especially when that means filling a last-minute order for some 600 perfectly executed pats. Setting aside esthetic considerations, butter shaping is also of practical value. "Why do I continue to shape my butter the old-fashioned way? Simply because a molding and wrapping machine, though certainly quicker, wouldn't give me the same flexibility when it comes to shape and response time. Not to mention that these machines also whiten butter and spoil its texture," says Jean-Yves. This is a man who will never adapt to life in the fast lane, always working at a leisurely pace for the sake of taste and elegance. A man who will always push the limits of bespoke marketing and produce new surprises – such as the stamps he has invented for certain customers. Bordier Butter can now be stamped with a particular motif or logo, recalling the days when the farmer's wife would use a wooden spoon to draw a flower, a cow, a bird or other design on the butter she sold at the market. "Butter might also be stamped with the seal or insignia of the local lord of the manor or some other notable figure, as a device to assert the status of the butter ... Like a label, only grander!"

## WRAPPING ...
## LONG LIVE
## PARCHMENT PAPER!

Wrapping, like every other stage of production, is an entirely manual process. Every bar of Bordier Butter is carefully wrapped by hand – and not just in any paper. Only parchment paper will do, this being the wrapper that replaced the cabbage leaf used for country butter before the 19th century. So why this loyalty to parchment paper? Because it is a part of the history of butter, doesn't tear when wet, feels nicer to the touch than aluminum foil but offers the same strength, and hugs the contours of whatever it encloses.

Bordier Butter embraces a plurality of butters. There are the Natural Tasting Butters, the Flavored Butters and the so-called "ephemeral" butters – some 15 in all. Jean-Yves Bordier is not out to break any records. He will not expand his portfolio at any price. He is simply driven by an insatiable curiosity to explore new avenues. Currently, his research focuses on salt and the possibility of producing butters containing salt from different sources, sea salt and also rock salt.

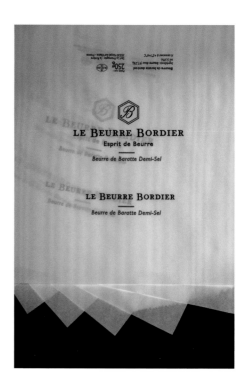

# The Bordier "Range"

"It would be a big mistake to spend all that time and energy creating delightful items for chefs, or 125g (4.4 oz) and 250g (8.8 oz) blocks for sale at markets and elsewhere, then wrap them in overly showy packaging," says Jean-Yves. "Bordier Butter", "Spirit of Butter" and "Churned Butter" are the only words that appear on the parchment paper used for Bordier Butter. Sober, elegant and understated – there is nothing loud about Bordier packaging. No trace of ostentatious marketing tactics. No shameless plugs for the particular source of a given sea salt or characteristics "rooted in terroir." For Jean-Yves Bordier and a growing coterie of aficionados, quality speaks for itself. There is no need of slogans, logos, labels or any other advertising ploy.

Custom-made butter for the French luxury cruise ship operator, PONANT

# Classic and Natural Tasting Butters

### CHURNED UNSALTED BUTTER

Grass, climate, the particular breed of cow, the farmer's handiwork – this butter perfectly exemplifies the idea of butter as Nature's blotting paper. Being an unsalted butter it is more fragile than its salted counterpart and thus absorbs the flavors and aromas of its terroir.

### CHURNED SEMI-SALTED BUTTER

The term "semi-salted" is used to distinguish butter containing no more than three percent salt. Adding salt to this sumptuous yet delicate-tasting butter gives it a vitality that exceeds the effects of the terroir and the season – the way the butter changes color and taste depending on the time of year and what the cows eat.

### CHURNED SALTED BUTTER

This is perhaps the most typically "Armorican" of the Bordier offerings. The one that best represents the salted butter that graced Brittany tables before plates were invented (a cliché maybe, but true). Back then, salt was added to keep the butter from spoiling. These days it's more a question of taste. The fine salt used by Jean-Yves produces a uniformly salted butter with just the right blend of saltiness and buttery flavor.

# Flavored Butter

In 1985 Jean-Yves Bordier slipped something other than salt into his butters, and since then his range of flavored butters has been an ever-evolving art. Originally invented as an aid to cooking, these unique butters have now far exceeded the original intention. They make a tantalizing starter to any meal, equally favored by ordinary folk and Michelin-starred chefs. What could be nicer than a small slice of bread with seaweed butter and a glass of white wine?

## CHURNED SEAWEED BUTTER

This is the first flavored butter ever created by Jean-Yves – butter with the taste of the sea par excellence. Even the color is surprising – those red, green and brown shades from the Dulse, Nori and Sea Lettuce seaweed collected off the coast of Finistère. That plus an incredible tang of the sea make this butter the perfect accompaniment to fish, seafood and shellfish but also (not so obvious) medium-rare beef.

## CHURNED
## YUZU
## BUTTER

This butter came on the scene in 2006 – at a time when yuzu was largely unknown in France. Yuzu citrus fruit is a cross between a wild mandarin orange and a lemon. Jean-Yves discovered it while traveling in Japan and came back with some yuzu powder and peel in his bags. Yuzu and lightly salted butter proved an inspired combination. Together they offer a harmonious blend of zingy freshness and subtle aromas of citrus that works wonders with fish, and also brings out the best in pastry recipes.

## CHURNED
## ESPELETTE
## CHILI BUTTER

Espelette Chili is emblematic of Basque cuisine. It comes from the village of Espelette itself and some dozen villages around it. After harvesting, the peppers are left to dry naturally hanging from the facades of houses, then ground to a power. This blend of butter and Espelette chili combines a deep orange color with just the right degree of heat to ramp up the flavor of mashed potatoes or rib of beef *à la plancha*.

## CHURNED LEMON-OLIVE OIL BUTTER

A miraculous coming-together that debunks preconceived notions about butter and olive oil not mixing. Jean-Yves got the idea for a lemon butter from the three-Michelin starred Guy Savoy, then heard about a Sicilian artisan who made lemon-infused olive oil. Tests showed that the silkiness of the butter and the freshness of the lemony olive oil were actually remarkably well matched, and Bordier lemon-olive oil butter was launched in 2010. Pair with lightly sautéed scallops or add to a vegetable *jardinière* just before serving to seal in the freshness.

## CHURNED SMOKED SALT BUTTER

A subtle but highly aromatic mix of salt, black pepper, roast onions and curry brings a lovely array of pungently smoky flavors to this butter. The recipe originated in Norway, based on an ancient local method for smoking salmon that was unearthed by French professional spice hunter and founder of *Terre Exotique*, Erwann de Kerros, who then shared his find with Jean-Yves. Pair with purées, white meat or slow-simmered vegetables.

## CHURNED GARLIC HERB BUTTER WITH SICHUAN PEPPER

In 2011, in response to popular demand from the chefs of leading Paris brasseries and other valued customers, Jean-Yves invented a garlic-and-herb butter. His stroke of genius was to add some Sichuan pepper, introducing a touch of menthol that tempered the garlicky notes. A new take on Maître d'Hotel Butter that enhances, but does not overwhelm, the flavor of meat.

### CHURNED SWEET MADAGASCAR
### VANILLA BUTTER

The pH of butter degrades vanilla ... Madagascar Vanilla is the exception, shown to be more resistant than the fabulous Tahitian Pure Vanilla that Jean-Yves discovered (and tested) thanks to pastry chef Gilles Marchal. This is seriously moreish butter, equally luscious on French Toast and pancakes, drizzled over baked apples or – why not – basted over poultry and fish just before they're done.

### CHURNED TAGINE
### SPICE BUTTER

The inspiration for this butter came from a summer barbecue with friends. Jean-Yves was enjoying a lamb brochette, and he felt it would be even better with a sprinkling of Moroccan spices. The very next morning he asked Erwann de Kerros to make him up some specific mixtures of spices. Testing was underway in the workshop by the following week. Cumin, coriander, paprika, lemon and cinnamon, plus other spices that must remain secret, combine to give this butter a pleasing whiff of Morocco.

### CHURNED TASMANIAN
### PEPPER BUTTER

This is another spice used by Jean-Yves: Tasmanian pepper, known for its medicinal properties and probably also used in aboriginal cooking. The berries and leaves are crushed to a fine powder, producing a powerful yet sensuous spice with a delicate piquancy. When combined with butter, this extraordinary spice delivers floral and fruit notes that make white meat and scallops even more delicious.

## CHURNED
## RASPBERRY BUTTER

A butter prompted by a desire for softness, sweetness, sensuous pleasure and freshness. No fruit satisfies that desire better than the raspberry, particularly when the sharpness of the fruit is mellowed by butter. This flavor-enhancing butter is equally suitable for use in savory or sweet dishes – red meat, crumbles or slow-simmered onions to go with a game terrine.

## CHURNED
## BUCKWHEAT BUTTER

Buckwheat is a robust herbaceous plant that originated in northern China before chance and circumstance brought it to the Armorican Massif. Buckwheat seeds (not "grains" because Buckwheat is not a cereal) are an energy food – highly nutritious and gluten free to boot. Jean-Yves toasts his Buckwheat seeds to bring out their nuttiness. He also only uses a selected variety of organic buckwheat, not the Chinese or Ukrainian buckwheat that makes up the other 99.9 percent of world production. Once a poor man's food and traditionally used to make buckwheat pancakes, buckwheat is now the gourmet ingredient behind this exceptional butter. Delicious on fish or white meat.

## NEW BUTTERS

Among the other butters that have come and gone over the years, one in particular is still remembered: Bordier Venezuela Cocoa Bean Butter. The cocoa beans are now also sourced from elsewhere in the world, under the expert guidance of leading French chocolatiers.

①
Wine Salt Butter

②
Raspberry Butter

③
Guérande Salt Powder Butter

④
Curcuma Butter

⑤
Tasmanian Pepper Butter

⑥
Cocoa Powder Butter

⑦
Sakura (Cherry Blossom) Butter

⑧
Espelette Chili Butter

⑨
Smoked Salt Butter

⑩
Seaweed Butter

⑪
Yuzu Butter

⑫
Sumac Pepper Butter

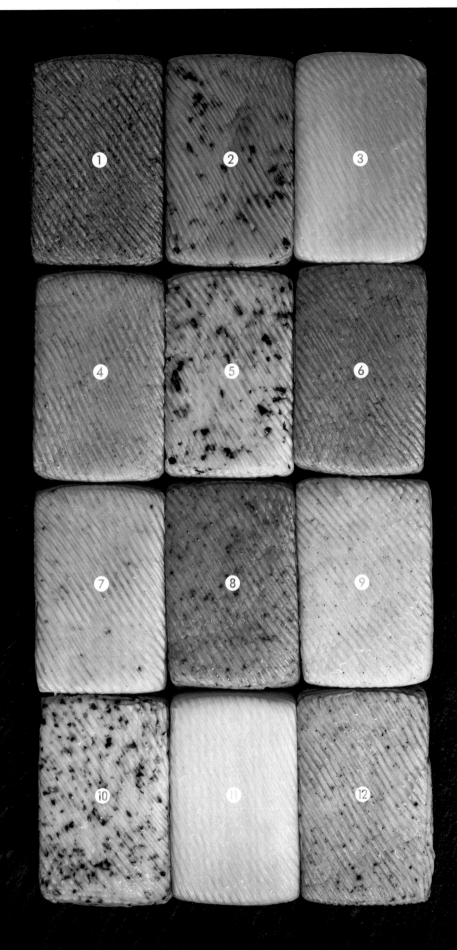

# THE SAGA OF
# SEAWEED BUTTER

One night in 1985 the fishmonger alongside the Maison du Beurre sold Jean-Yves Bordier a magnificent brill. The beast was placed on a bed of seaweed. Before the two bottles of white wine served with the appetizer and the main dish, Jean-Yves had the idea of making a *duxelle* with the seaweed and mixing in some of his semi-salted butter. As he took the brill from the oven, he topped the hot filets with seaweed butter, which melted into the flesh of the fish releasing its briny aroma. Sheer bliss ... Seaweed and butter turned out to be a heavenly combination! Thanks to Jean-Yves' culinary improvisation, the butter took on an iodine tang of the sea. And with that, seaweed butter was born.

Jean-Yves had just unwittingly invented what was destined to be one of his company's flagship products. For many years he only made seaweed butter for his friends, using a mixing bowl not the kneader (seaweed and kneading make poor bedfellows – see below). In fact, it took a lot of hard work and determination to arrive at a recipe that fitted the bill – that is, met EU food safety standards but contained no preservative. The turning point came in December 1999, at the Salon des Saveurs in Paris. On the Friday, the Bordier team had the pleasure of a visit from *Les Echos* journalist Jean-Louis Galesne. He came to buy some semi-salted butter and, hopefully, something "original"

that he could show to his gourmet friends at lunchtime. Jean-Yves said he had just the thing: "There's just a bit of our seaweed butter left, about 300 grams (10 ounces) – delicious but not easy to make because the little black seeds make a real mess of the churn, get lodged in the wooden staves. So we only produce it in small quantities and keep quiet about it."

First thing Monday morning Jean-Yves received a call from Eric Lecerf, sous-chef to three-Michelin starred chef Joël Robuchon. It was about their regular order for Bordier Butter, which they used in all kinds of dishes but especially in Robuchon's dreamy mash potatoes. "Good morning Monsieur Bordier, said Lecerf. "What's this I hear about you keeping things to yourself? How come you never told us about this fabulous seaweed butter of yours that Jean-Louis brought back with him? The chef wants to place an order for some next week ... Difficult to make in large quantities, you say? Well, you'd better find a way because he plans to add it to the menu as soon as possible." It was as if someone had thrown a switch. Jean-Yves armed himself with a kneading trough and fulfilled Joël Robuchon's order. By 2003 he was supplying all of Robuchon's ateliers and had launched his seaweed butter into the market far beyond St. Malo. The rest as they say is history. The butter was a roaring success and spawned a raft of imitations.

LE BEURRE BORDIER
Beurre de Baratte aux Algues
LE BEURRE BORDIER
Beurre de Baratte aux Algues
Esprit de beurre
Beurre de Baratte aux Algues
LE BEURRE BORDIER
Beurre de Baratte aux Algues

# BORDIER

## A DECISIVE MEETING

**JEAN-YVES BORDIER**

One night in October 1986, famous French cheese maker Pierre Androuët and his gourmet friend Jean-Guy Fontaine invited the little world of Brittany cheese makers to a restaurant in Rennes. Their objective? To form a guild of French cheese makers based in Brittany

As a young butter and cheese maker at the time, I was far from sure of myself. But the couple sitting beside me at the table, Jean and Françoise Clanchin, did a lot to build my confidence. Jean Clanchin with his offbeat humor and entrenched positions was enough to make anyone laugh. His wife Françoise, a graduate of the French National Dairy School (ENIL), was equally full of fun but shifted

back to professional mode when the conversation took a more serious turn. In 1961 the ENIL was an all-male school so Françoise had to obtain special permission to attend classes. She combined a high level of expertise with an incredible capacity for analytical listening and anyone could see that this was a woman going places.

The couple were married in 1964 and formed a formidable double-act from the start, adopting the slogan "Tradition and Innovation" for their newly founded Triballat business. In 1968 they launched the first sterilized milk bottle sealed by a plastic capsule. By 1975, Françoise had persuaded several milk producers in the Ille-et-Vilaine department to convert to livestock farming and feeding practices consistent with the principles of organic agriculture (*bio* in French). In 1989 she and Jean-Marc Levêque submitted the first terms of reference for the production of organic milk – an unprecedented step that drew skepticism from their fellow professionals. Nearly 45 years later, an overwhelming majority of dairy producers in France make organic claims but only Triballat's Vrai brand is legitimately entitled to call itself *bio*.

Triballat became a pioneer of the organic movement and left its mark on the history of milk. In 1986 its research into soya proteins culminated in the launch of the first plant-based yoghurt, with Sojasun being released as Triballat's flagship brand two years later.

In just a few years, Françoise and Jean Clanchin proved themselves Captains of Industry.

Françoise's visionary thinking was built into Triballat's corporate DNA and also into the life of her hometown, Noyal-sur-Vilaine in Brittany, where she served as mayor from 1995 to 2008, displaying a high level of civic engagement.

In February 1998, I heard from a Normandy cheese maker called Denis Thébaut that a Triballat subsidiary was interested in my work as a cheese and butter maker. Madame Clanchin invited me to join the firm in a consultative capacity. Eighteen months later we reached an agreement. October 1999 then marked a turning point for both of us. Françoise Clanchin was fascinated by my work with butter, as you might expect of a woman who like her fellow students at the ENIL in Surgères lived up to the nickname *babigeote* – marshland patois for buttermilk and by extension, all of the butter makers in the Vendée and Charente regions. Madame Clanchin loved butter and set out to prove it. At a time when the production of high quality milk was falling by the wayside, the revival of traditional butter-making seemed entirely sensible to her. She gave me her overwhelming support and in January 2005 we moved the buttery from St. Malo to Triballat's premises in Noyal-sur-Vilaine.

Just imagine: two hundred square meters of space entirely devoted to butter! A busy workshop complete with kneaders straight out of the 19th century plus more than 25 "pounders" – men and women who, like their 17th century counterparts, hand-shape the newly-churned butter to keep its texture intact. We employ proportionately more staff than any other dairy business. So whatever our detractors may say, we don't just make good butter we also have a social impact. Françoise Clanchin was one of the first to realize that I had managed to create butter with a pedigree – something it lost in the great battle over healthy eating. I certainly didn't see that coming when I started out. Today she takes pride in having recreated a traditional buttery within an environment equipped with cutting-edge technologies. She can supply demands for plant-based proteins such as hemp, the while safeguarding the traditions that have made Bordier Butter the benchmark for connoisseurs everywhere.

I share her pride – proud to have shared an adventure with a woman who has taught me so much. Her son Olivier Clanchin, President of Triballat, is certain to steer the fortunes of Bordier Butter and cheese with unerring aplomb. It's not often in life that you meet exceptional people. Women like Madame Monique Bouygues, a discreet presence who left her mark on my life, gently encouraging me to stand by my convictions. Also Madame Roxane Dubuisson, who galvanized me into bringing my butter to the attention of top chefs.

I have been fortunate indeed in having three good fairies to watch over me. Life has been good to me but I know that Bordier Butter would never have taken shape without the extraordinary vision of Françoise Clanchin, who I thank from the bottom of my heart.

We had our differences of course, as happens in any business, but there was always enormous respect between us. What we shared is something I wish for anyone who lives life to the full.

Fanfan, it's been a thrill! THANK YOU.

# THE WORLD
## *of Jean-Yves Bordier*

It is true that the butter is no longer kneaded here, and the
cheeses are now finished elsewhere ... But it is here within
the noble walls of one of St. Malo's oldest houses that you
feel the heartbeat of "Planet" Bordier.

# Home is *St. Malo!*

## LA MAISON DU BEURRE

Jean-Yves came to the Rue de l'Orme one day in 1985 to take over La Maison du Beurre that was created in 1927, and has never left this little patch of sloping cobblestone, the most foodie lane in the walled quarter. Thirty years later, he cannot go more than two meters without shaking the hand of an established customer or kissing the mother of a family whose children have grown up on Bordier foodstuffs. His products enjoy an international reputation, but Jean-Yves' roots are in St. Malo, now and forever!
In 2008, La Maison du Beurre got a gentle facelift, to hide her wrinkles without in any way destroying her soul, to make her walls a lighter color, while retaining her period shop fascia and those magnificent tiles by the famous artist Odorico.

## THE BUTTER MUSEUM

Since 2008, La Maison du Beurre has featured a little butter museum, conceived by Michel Phélizon: not a *musaillon* knocked together in a hurry, but 20m2 of attractive museography that displays a range of tools, including old churns, and an outstanding set of information panels that tell the history of butter, from its origins to the French butter of today, describing along the way the part it has played in cooking, its place in society across the centuries, how you conserve butter, how you make butter, and of course the particular qualities of Bordier Butter. This is a museum that provides an insightful presentation of butter, a place not to be missed after you have filled your shopping basket with butters and well-ripened cheeses, prime charcuterie and butterscotch, and La Quiberonnaise sardines in Bordier Butter.

**THE BUTTER MUSEUM**

A space like no other in France!
The saga of butter from Neolithic
times to the present day. This
space embodies the vision
of Françoise Clanchin, the
erudition of historian Michel
Phélizon and the passion of
Jean-Yves Bordier for a foodstuff
with extraordinary potential.

## THE BISTRO
## AUTOUR DU BEURRE

Why add a restaurant? "I wanted to achieve three things here. I wanted a place that would make the connection between the pitchfork and the table fork. A place that would allow me to be at the farm for milking at dawn, then spend the morning making the butter. And I wanted somewhere where customers could discover a light style of cooking with Bordier Butter, where I could demonstrate to journalists the sound foundation on which my business is built," explains Jean-Yves Bordier. The Bistro Autour du Beurre opened in 2011, alongside the historic shop in the Rue de l'Orme, and effortlessly established itself as one of St. Malo's best restaurants. And it isn't hard to see why! Ancient and modern come together in a delightful decor of old stone and designer furniture, raw materials and oddments scavenged from old dairies, such as that most important thing of all, a churn – unearthed by chance in Belgium – now reinvented as a dining table. Under the talented baton of Steve Delamaire, the nuanced menu tells a story of local produce, seasonal offerings at their freshest, inshore fishing and fine fish just landed from local waters. Not to mention the butters that embellish

the *amuse-bouche* and flatter the chef's recipes: a little seaweed butter slipped into a purée, a touch of yuzu butter to liven up a fish sauce. A smiling welcome and a short but appropriate wine list do the rest.

## THE FROMAGÉE
## JEAN-YVES BORDIER

Established in 2007, this gourmet grocery in the Courtoisville district, not far from Sillon beach in St. Malo, eases crowding at the original Maison du Beurre inside the town walls, especially in summer. Natural and flavored butters, some 200 kinds of cheese, milk-based desserts, deli fare, wine ... The whole Bordier range just begging to fill your basket.

### AUTOUR DU BEURRE

A relaxed and thoughtful
restaurant, in the spirit of the Alain
Kruger broadcast *On ne parle pas
la bouche pleine!.* (You don't speak
with your mouth full.) The decor is
the work of that excellent architect
Hervé Perrin – elegant lines that
combine simplicity and modernity.

## THE PLACE
## GOURMANDE

Place Gourmande at the entrance to St. Malo has all that a lively clientele requires. This modern and innovative covered market houses six first-quality food outlets: the outstanding butcher Maurice, the fishmonger Chez Françoise, the Maison Dreux for fruit and vegetables, the Caves du Coin for a fine selection of wines, the Augustin bakery and … the Fromagée Jean-Yves Bordier for butter, cheese and everything else.

## COMPANIONS IN TASTE:
## THE INTIMATE ST. MALO
## WORLD OF JEAN-YVES
## BORDIER

In the course of his career, Jean-Yves Bordier has forged a number of indestructible friendships based on a shared commitment to good produce. Here he introduces us to some of his dearest companions, those who gravitate to his St. Malo hideout. "Culinary professions have this capacity to form intense personal relationships. In my line of business I come into contact with a huge range

of people and, with some of them, something special happens. Something to do with the way they taste foods, react to foods, form their own opinions uncolored by preconceptions. With my non-professional friends, what we say and feel comes from the heart – it's spontaneous, freethinking. The words might be crude but the opinion is often spot-on.

When the winter tides come to the Chausey Islands, we hold various tasting events at my friend Christophe Bizeul's place. Lots of shellfish and fish, mainly thanks to Gilles Guinemer, the Rue de l'Orme's fisherman and fishmonger extraordinaire – so plenty of opportunity for our amateur, but no less talented, cooks to be creative. Things get really exciting if Yves Camdeborde or Jacques Ferrandez happen to drop by.

"Drinks in hand, we dream up recipes at the Petite Cale restaurant, Massu's place, with Jean-Thom and Jean Pinou, François, Christian, Patrick, Fred, Stéphane and Fabrice officiating, watched over by 'Yellow Dog' Jean-Pierre and *Phi-Phi* our *Burgermeister* and fishing supervisor. Then there are the professionals amongst us. There's Yannick Heude, sommelier and owner

**COMPANIONS IN TASTE**

The pleasure of meeting up with Morgan and Thibault Hector at their Café de l'Ouest or their Lion d'Or brasserie. A group of professional friends and food-lovers who would have made good subjects for cartoonist Jacques Ferrandez' *Frères de Terroirs*.

## The world of Jean-Yves Bordier

A *Kouign-Amann* (traditional Breton cake made with bread dough) at La Maison du Pain, Rue de l'Orme, St. Malo.

"Here, taste this," he says – those three little words so dear to our hearts.

of the Caves de l'Abbaye Saint-Jean in St. Malo. It was his idea to form a group of *artisans du goût* (craftsmen of taste) committed to passing on their passion and knowledge. From that came the School of Taste, *L'Ecole du Goût*. We have two chefs, Luc Mobihan from the starred Le Saint Placide restaurant in St. Malo, and Olivier Gousset from Zag in Dinan, plus the baker-patissier Philippe Renault, macaroon champion of France in 2015, and of course Yannick Heude, a gifted discoverer of outstanding winemakers, plus yours truly. In addition to our two-hourly tasting classes, we organize one-off events, joint projects with hotel schools, cooking contests and gourmet food shows.

"Pleasure and sharing are what make my life in St. Malo such a thrill. The pleasure of being part of a group, of going to collect a *pluma* made by Raphaël at Olivier Ruellan's deli store, or heading for a table at Arnaud Béruel's Bénétin restaurant to feast on abalone prepared with seaweed butter as we take in the spectacular view over St. Malo Bay and Chausey. Meetings like these are a real joy, not least for Bernard Larcher of Breizh Café who often turns up at the Rue de l'Orme with some unknown (and invariably delicious) cider he wants me to taste. 'Here, taste this', he says – those three little words so dear to our hearts."

# BREIZH CAFÉ

## AND BERTRAND LARCHER

"To understand Breizh Café, you must first understand where I come from!" And so begins *Breizh Café, 60 Recettes Autour des Produits du Terroir Breton*, a book dedicated to the incredible story of Bertrand Larcher, a native of Brittany who set off to explore the world and eventually opened pancake houses and outlets in Brittany (Cancale and St. Malo), Paris and Japan.

None of this would have been possible without the fresh, wholesome produce of his Brittany terroir. There is the butter that he uses to grease his crepe maker. Not just any old butter but the ingredient that ensures the batter is cooked "just right". There are the buckwheat and organic wheat that go to make the batter itself. Then there are all those other products, including the buttermilk, chitterling sausages, lard, oysters and pot-caught spider crabs – and not forgetting cider, the Celtic drink par excellence. Produced by talented cider-makers, Brittany cider offers an extraordinary blend of complexity and elegance. But it is only now, thanks to Bertrand Larcher, that it is finally getting the respect it deserves. Bertrand is a champion of good food, and an eloquent advocate for this land of ours and its reputation for top quality produce. He promotes a local savoir-faire that never yields to market forces.

Another core element of Bertrand's life and work is the link between his native Brittany culture and his adoptive Japanese culture. The two come together in Bertrand. He brings that keen eye for detail so typical of Nippon society to pursue traditional crepe-making in its purest form. He uses seaweed in his cooking just as they have been doing in Japan for centuries, and here in France for the past few years. He adds a touch of Yuzu vinegar to Cancale oysters in much the same way as I add yuzu to my butter. The bridge between the two cultures is buckwheat, which we use to make pancakes and the Japanese use to make their famous soba noodles. As it happens, Bertrand is also the owner of the Maison du Sarrasin in St. Malo.

Bertrand does in fact draw his energy and imagination from childhood. Fond memories of the butter made

on his parents' farm and in the neighbors' butter churn. Of watching the sales lady at the *épicerie-bistrot* (grocery-cum-eatery) on the Place du Marché in Fougères carve out chunks of butter for each customer then pat them into shape. Of turning up every Thursday to proffer his jar for filling with butter just as the workmen from the Nazart dairy were delivering jars of their own!

"On public holidays, mom would make a huge dish of buttery mash. She would create a well in the center for a big slug of butter, then surround the mash with slices of smoking Andouille sausage. The meat had that smell of hay, that whiff of homemade stock. To finish off the meal, she would prepare Pippin apples baked in sugar and butter on a wood-fired stove. A real treat! Dad wanted me to become a farmer but I preferred to go into the world of hotels and catering. But some day I'll have a farm where my children and relatives can come and stay. That way I will have come full circle. My life is to share and pass down, keep memories alive and entrust those memories to my children just as I bring them to my work!" And there you have it. Bertrand Larcher is a man worth getting to know. A generous friend, the mastermind behind the tagline La Crêpe Autrement (a different take on crepes) and the talented inventor of those blissfully delicious and endlessly surprising Breizh rolls!

Thank you Bertrand!

# Bordier: a reputation that reaches far beyond the walls of St. Malo!

## BORDIER BUTTERS TO TAKE HOME

So where can you buy Bordier Butter? Outside St. Malo, Bordier Butter owns a stall titled La Fromagée in Rennes central market, La Criée, and operates sales outlets inside leading Brittany wine merchants: the Cellier Fougerais in Fougères, Côté Vignoble in Dol-de-Bretagne, the Cave des Sommeliers in Douarnenez, and the 3 Comptoirs wine bar in Vitré. Far beyond Armorican borders, Bordier products also fill the windows of the best *crèmeries* in Paris and in France as a whole, not counting top grocery stores such as Lafayette Gourmet and La Grande Épicerie de Paris in the capital.

## BORDIER BUTTER IN RESTAURANTS: CUSTOM-MADE FOR THE GREAT CHEFS OF THE WORLD!

From luxury hotel bistros to wine bars and gastronomic eateries, in Brittany, Paris, Japan, Dubai, Bangkok and elsewhere ... the number of places that carry Bordier butters and cheeses is virtually endless. And there's a long waiting list. Frédéric Meyer, French gastronome, owner of five restaurants in Bangkok and a food purist with the best food connections in the world, had to wait a whole year. Jean-Yves Bordier is not a man to put quantity before quality. For the sake of his soul, his savoir-faire and his reputation for excellence, he prefers to turn down orders rather than increase the rate and volume of production. Whether served in a bistro alongside an unpretentious platter of cold cuts or presented under glass in luxury hotels, Bordier Butter must be the same for everybody ... or almost. Because there are also the couture butters, those specially made for the great chefs of famed restaurants, adjusting the shape, the weight and even the degree of salt according to the requirements of the customer. Some even have personalized stamps, maybe with a design that reflects the initials of the celebrated client in question.

# THE HISTORY OF THE CRÉMERIES

MICHEL PHÉLIZON

Dairy stores as we know them today are a relatively recent invention. For centuries, French farmers sold their meager output of milk, butter and cheese at the market in their neighboring town. Big towns did not represent a big enough market to justify specialized outlets, unlike products such as meat and fish or fruit and vegetables. The market for milk and to a lesser extent butter was handled by *laitières* who collected milk from farms close to urban centers and sold it from street barrows. They also sold whatever butter and cheese they had to hand.

The 19th century then brought a craze for *café au lait* in the morning – and with that, the demand for milk exploded. Milk depots appeared on the outskirts of towns, supplied by increasingly distant milk producers. *Vacheries*, a kind of zero-grazing dairy farm, meanwhile developed inside towns, numbering 464 in 1867 in Paris proper, and 612 twenty years later in the immediate vicinity of the capital. Home milk deliveries started, and the first *crémeries-fromageries* appeared – a form of establishment that was struggling to find its place in the market. This is evidenced by an entry in Pierre Larousse's *Grand Dictionnaire Universel du XIXᵉ Siècle* (1863) that was later quoted by Claire Delfosse in *Le Métier de Crémier-Fromager de 1850 à Nos Jours* (Mer du Nord, 2014): "For several years the word *crémerie* has denoted establishments that stand somewhere between a restaurant and a café, where everything except cream is sold – essentially a workman's cafe, where milk pudding, café à la crème, chocolate, pork chops and eggs are pretty much the dominant dishes." Most *crèmeries* then moved over to selling milk, butter, eggs and cheese, and also in most cases vegetables, fruit and other perishable foodstuffs. Eventually the local *crèmerie* formed part of the urban landscape like the baker and the butcher.

Then came competition from franchised grocery stores, as started by Félix Potin, and points of sale opened by capital-rich industrial dairies – Maggie, Hauser, Société

Laitière Moderne, Gervais, etc. The *crémeries-fromageries* tried to fight back by forming professional unions and opting for the sale of butter, eggs and especially cheeses. They became "hyperspecialists", like the luxury grocery stores that developed between the two wars, forming a link of sorts between the small producer and the customer. The *crémeries-fromageries* depended on the large-scale market for a part of their stock – in the Paris central market, two stalls in twelve were devote to butter, eggs and cheese – but they also bought directly from farm producers. The 1960s then saw changes in the countryside as large-scale distribution came to France. It was a period driven by practical objectives, helped by the longer shelf life of foods and product diversification. It was the era of marketing, publicity and brands.

Would the *crémeries-fromageries* disappear like the local grocery stores?, watching helplessly as their ever-decreasing share in sales of household milk products dwindled to nothing? Not a bit of it. *Crémiers/fromagers* like Nicole Barthélémy and Martine Dubois completely changed the game in the 2000s, responding to growing consumer demand for quality, authenticity and naturalness. Their fellow professionals rose to the occasion, and French cheese-makers are now among the laureates of the *Meilleurs Ouvriers de France* – a title awarded ever year to the best artisans in France. Many of these award-winning *fromagers-affineurs* (cheesemonger/finishers) now own stores in Paris and other French towns. They include Marie Quatrehomme and Laurent Dubois, plus other well-known figures who shook up the industry, among them Roland Barthélémy, Philippe Olivier, Eric Lefebvre, Claude Maret and Hervé Mons. Following in their footsteps is a new generation of dedicated *fromager-affineur* that can rightly claim the title "master craftsman". "The revival is also being driven by the arrival of passionate food enthusiasts – people driven out of their jobs by the economic crisis, who then invested their severance pay in training, a cheese-making tour of France and eventually their own cheese store or deli store," explains Jean-Yves. "People with a real enthusiasm for their work, sometimes couples, sometimes members of small teams, but all of them customers for Bordier Butter and the best ambassadors we could wish for, ever ready to give consumers the benefit of their expertise."

# - 2 -

# BORDIER,
## BUTTER
## IN GASTRONOMY

# A HISTORICAL
# *perspective*

## Butter, foundation of French cuisine

**TEXT BY MICHEL PHÉLIZON**

"In Paris butter is used in the preparation of entrees and nearly all desserts; nothing is made with hot oil, the taste being generally unsuited to the Parisian palate." So wrote Grimod de la Reynière in 1812 in his *Almanach des Gourmands*. An extreme view certainly, based solely on *haute cuisine* – elitist cuisine for the moneyed upper classes, not everyday cooking for the working classes or what we know today as the middle class. But a revealing view all the same, since it testifies to that extraordinary fondness for butter that characterized the culinary revolution in France (and elsewhere) between the 16th and 18th centuries. As French historian Jean-Louis Flandrin noted: "The increasing use of butter in cookery books is one of the major changes of the modern era." So why this sudden enthusiasm for butter? Partly to rediscover the tastes of foods, not disguise them with sour, spicy or sugary sauces, butter being a fantastic flavor enhancer. But mainly in response to the growing awareness of the versatility of butter, which in turn fuelled culinary creativity. Butter opened up all kinds of possibilities. It could be used to fry, roast, sauté, brown, crystallize, sweat vegetables and keep food from sticking. It could be used as an emulsifier in sauces. And most especially it could be used in pastry making, which took off in the 19th century with the arrival of sugar (cane sugar followed by beet sugar). I do not propose to reel off all the recipes that have left their mark on French cuisine, even less attribute them to any single chef or culinary writer as most have been reworked over

the years. But it is worth pausing to consider sauces and patisserie. Turning first to sauces, Auguste Escoffier offered this opinion in his cookbook *Le Guide Culinaire* (1903): "Sauces are the most important part of cooking. It is sauces that propelled French cuisine to fame and sauces that ensure it reigns supreme to this day." Notable examples include roux, a blend of flour and butter, and its derivative Béchamel sauce; also Béarnaise sauce. As regards patisserie, there are so many butter-based techniques that it's hard to know where to start. The most obvious examples are *pâte brisée* (shortcrust pastry), *pâte sablée* (shortbread dough) and *pâte feuilletée* (puff pastry). But there is also brioche dough and choux pastry, *mille-feuille*, Brittany butter cake (*gâteau Breton*) butter-enriched sponge cake (*gâteau manqué*, a 19th century invention), and all those other cakes and delicacies that appeared in the 20th century: chocolate cake, Genoise, classic pound cake (*quatre-quarts*) and madeleine cupcakes.

Let's hear it too for the humble slice of bread and butter – a treat dear to the heart of the Marquise de Sévigné, as shown in this letter to Madame de

# " ... a slab of freshly made butter, still oozing with milky tear drops under the knife "

Grignan (1690): "I love that goodly Prévalaye butter they bring us every week. I love it and eat it like a Brittany girl. Bread and butter is always a treat [...] just begging to be sprinkled with *fines herbes* and violets." French writer Colette likewise waxes lyrical about butter in 1930: "my *gourmandize* is of rustic origin [...] a twelve pound loaf of dark country bread [...] and a slab of freshly made butter, still oozing with milky tear drops under the knife [...] hand-pressed, rancid after two days, as perfumed, as ephemeral as a flower – luxury butter." Not forgetting, of course, that great Parisian classic *jambon-beurre-cornichon* without which, wrote Cristian Millau in his *Petit Dictionnaire Amoureux de la Gastronomie*, "Paris would not be Paris." Butter has given us some of the most emblematic dishes in the French culinary repertory and remains pivotal to their success today – on condition

that it is of the very highest quality. As noted in 1867 by French chef Jules Gouffé in his *Le Livre de Cuisine*: "A small quantity of sweet butter will improve any preparation where it is required. Whereas with bad butter, the result will be exactly the reverse: the more you add of it, the worse your dish will become."

And there you have it, dear readers. Adding just the right amount of butter is apparently the secret to cooking French-style: cooking in the grand tradition, as practiced by French housewives and popularized from the second half of the 19th century onward. "Butter is to French cuisine what the sun is to plants," wrote A.B. de Périgord in 1852 in his *Le Trésor de la Cuisinière et de la Maîtresse de Maison*. A somewhat quaint aphorism certainly, but no less true because of it.

# Flavored butters in the classical tradition of French gastronomy

**TEXT BY MICHEL PHÉLIZON AND JEAN-YVES BORDIER**

Butter is a flavor enhancer: it increases the perceived intensity of the taste and smell of food. The same is true of all fats and lipids, which have been used as flavor enhancers since time immemorial.

So it is hardly surprising to find that the practice of flavoring butters with aromatic plants can be traced back at least to the Middle Ages. The following centuries then saw it enter the classic French culinary repertory.

Take for instance, this detailed recipe in *Les Remèdes Charitables de Madame Fouquet* (1682): "In May and September, lay in a provision of butter; salt it well; take thyme, marjoram, chives and onions, chop them as finely as possible then work them well into the butter, adding salt as you go, and the butter will impart their flavor to the soups. So much for poor people. For more delicate palates, do as they do in the Lorraine. Take freshly melted butter, add the aforementioned herbs, leave to cool then salt the butter well and place in clay pots or pine containers. This cooked butter will not taste strong; it is good for soups and fried food."

Flavored butters grew ever more varied and ever more elaborate throughout the 18th and 19th centuries. They added refinement to any dish and became a cherished ingredient of bourgeois French cuisine in particular and regional cooking in particular. French chef and author Prosper Montagné gives this definition of flavored butters in his *Larousse Gastronomique* (1938):

"A term used to describe butters containing added substances that are usually minced or purée; and butters cooked to varying degrees or simply melted, seasoned with condiments, served as an accompaniment to fish, meat and vegetables. Flavored butters in the first category are used either as a complementary element in sauces and other preparations, or as an auxiliary ingredient in the making of cold dishes, or as garnish for cold *hors-d'oeuvre*."

There follows a description of some 50 different preparations for use as stand-alone ingredients, or as

seasonings or in cooking. Examples range from the inevitable Maître d'Hôtel butter (flavored with parsley, pepper, fine salt and lemon juice) to garlic butter, anchovy butter, lemon butter, scallion butter and other far more elaborate creations. Among these are Chivry butter (flavored with parsley, tarragon, chervil, pimpernel, chives and scallions) and Montpellier Butter (flavored with parsley, chervil, watercress, tarragon, chives, spinach, gherkins, capers, anchovy filets, garlic and olive oil).

From the 1960s onward most of these butters gradually disappeared from cook books, partly because a lighter cuisine was now in vogue but mainly because of the difficulty of obtaining fresh herbs in town – that, and the shift toward less laborious meal preparation.

Then along came Bordier Flavored Butters – hand crafted butters that take the butter-flavoring tradition to a new level, with new recipes, created with the help of all-star chefs for discerning food lovers, ready for use as an ingredient in cooking or as a table butter.

# Qualities and uses of Bordier Butters

*Butter is the cornerstone of our cooking and our heritage.
It gives backbone to flavor and imparts creaminess to texture.*

Hugues Pouget, Pâtissier Hugo et Victor

# BREAD AND BUTTER

### STEVEN L. KAPLAN

Bread and butter form a couple, and just like other couples, they have their difficulties. Historically speaking, bread and butter only became an item quite recently. Bread is a staple food, essential to the survival of most people in Europe and elsewhere. It is above all associated with that vast swathe of society that we call "the working classes" – people with simple lifestyles and few material resources who subsist on cereals. For most French working class families in urban and rural areas, butter remained a luxury until at least the early 1900s (France itself being divided into areas that produced butter, lard or oil). Butter was the preserve of an elite, as illustrated by the contest launched in 1869 by the righteous Napoleon III offering a prize to anyone who could produce a low-cost fat resembling that most prized of staples, butter.

This class distinction showed in the language of the street. Butter conjured up notions of opulence, of a rich, nourishing food loaded with flavor, fat and calories. It spawned eloquent expressions for making money (*faire son beurre*) and moving forward in life (*beurrer son pain* – literally "buttering your bread"). Butter became a metaphor for earning more, eating better and, in a word, living better. Working-class consumers in French dairy-farming regions fantasized about eating butter and sinking their teeth into freshly baked bread (white, naturally). For them like most other consumers, bread and butter was a figment of the imagination long before it became a reality. Today the working classes still regard the bread and butter on their table as a dream come true. For them, less blasé perhaps than their richer counterparts, bread and butter represents a triumph of hedonism over social discrimination.

Bread and butter came earlier to the United States. The idea took hold in the early 19th century, reflecting the collective image of a land of plenty (rather than penury) and a country that prided itself on being the world's most egalitarian society. Whether it fulfilled a basic need for food or survival in general, bread and butter quickly became commonplace. The Americans, like the French and other nationalities, turned the wish into a reality and made bread and butter a part of their everyday lives. Such an integral part of life that in France we coined the phrase *être comme pain et beurre* to describe the things or people that go together – always a favorite expression of mine. For me, breaking bread with friends is a form of profane communion, a way of forging and strengthening the ties between us. It is a ritual we perform in a spirit of sharing. The butter that now invariably accompanies that bread reinforces those ties and deepens the sense of sharing. It joins with the bread just as the people around the table join with each other in partaking of the bread and butter. "Buttered bread cannot be unbuttered" anymore than those people around the table can undo what they have just done. Their shared enjoyment of the combined flavors of bread and butter binds them socially, emotionally and sensually. It is a magical moment of pleasure and conviviality that they will think about every time they (re)eat good crusty bread topped with lovingly churned butter. A memory-laden moment that is to them what the madeleine was to Marcel Proust. Then there is the metaphorical significance of bread and butter – a famously devoted couple (you could almost call them accomplices) whose cognitive impact extends far beyond the table. Bread and butter represent a benchmark, a reference against which other things can be measured. They help us to make sense of the world around us, precisely because they are so basic, so visceral, so much a part of our experience yet also so much more than that. No-one ever said it better than the American poet James Russell Lowell (1818-1891):

"Not a deed would he do
Not a word would he utter
Till he's weighed its relation
To plain bread and butter."

**BY ERIC BRIFFARD,**
*MEILLEUR OUVRIER DE FRANCE,*
**EXECUTIVE CHEF AND CULINARY**
**ARTS DIRECTOR AT THE CORDON**
**BLEU SCHOOL, PARIS**

# Clarified butter

## WHY CLARIFY BUTTER?

Clarified butter is butter with all of its water and milk solids (whey proteins) removed. Whey is the component in butter that burns and turns black when cooked, leaving carbon as a residue. Scientists have shown that whey is carcinogenic when eaten on a daily basis. Clarified butter can be heated to a much higher temperature than ordinary butter, making it more suitable for sauté-ing, frying and roasting.

Dice a 250-gram/half pound stick of fresh butter (the larger the quantity, the easier it is to clarify).

Heat the butter in a saucepan or double-boiler over a low heat until completely melted.

Pour your newly melted butter into a container and skim off the foamy white layer that forms on the surface with the aid of a spoon or straining spoon. For added purity, lay a sheet of kitchen roll on top of the butter then lift it sharply away to remove any residue.

What remains now is clear, golden, clarified butter. Use a spoon or small ladle to transfer it to a bowl or jar, being careful not stir up the whey that remains at the bottom of the pan.

That's all there is to it. The clarified butter is then ready for immediate use or can be kept in the refrigerator for 2-3 weeks – which is a big plus.

*Chef's tip: you can of course use fresh butter to sauté meat or fish (sole meunière, for instance) – on condition that you turn the heat right down and baste regularly with a spoon so that the butter keeps foaming. The ideal temperature is 140°-150°C (275°-300°F) – any higher than that and the butter will burn.*

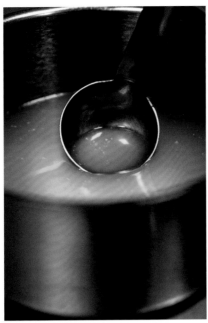

## HOW TO USE
## CLARIFIED BUTTER

---

### IN COOKING:

Clarified butter is ideal for roasting
and browning (fish, chicken, meat),
sauté-ing (potatoes) and frying. It
retains all the taste of butter but
where regular butter would burn
and taste bitter, clarified butter does
not. So no risk of those little black
specks of casein.

### IN SAUCES:

Clarified butter can be used for
all kinds of emulsified sauces.
Hollandaise and Béarnaise
Sauce, Sauce Maltaise and French
Mousseline sauce are all made by
creating a sabayon, heating the
egg yokes until they thicken as you
drizzle in the clarified butter to form
an emulsion.

### IN FLAVORED
### INFUSIONS:

Heat the clarified butter to 50°-60°C
(122°-140° F) then infuse with spices
to taste – curry powder, caraway,
cardamom, turmeric, cloves,
cinnamon, coriander, cumin, fennel
or mustard seeds, paprika, pepper
grains, red pepper (dried), star anise –
whatever takes your fancy.
Proceed the same way for aromatic
herbs – thyme, rosemary, bay leaves,
oregano, basil – and other flavorings:
citrus zest (lemon, mandarin, yuzu,
citron); dried mushrooms (porcini
or morel mushrooms); and rhizomes
(turmeric, ginger, galangal).

# *Lier*
## (to thicken),
**BY YVES CAMDEBORDE**

### THE MEANING OF *LIER*

In the French culinary vocabulary, *lier* is the process that brings smoothness to a liquid and gives it texture. Because a liquid can have a texture. Butter will do that – add smoothness and texture. And because it is a fantastic flavor enhancer, it will also add taste. These days we use a lot less butter than before, to avoid any heaviness, but we still use butter just the same.

### WHAT FOODS BENEFIT FROM A *LIAISON* OF BUTTER?

All kinds of white meat, poultry, offal such as calf sweetbreads and foods with a taste of the sea – mussels for instance. Using the butter to thicken the juices brings out the flavor without changing it.

### HOW TO MAKE A SUCCESSFUL *LIAISON* OF BUTTER

Butter should be added at the last moment, just before serving. With calf sweetbreads for instance, after deglazing the pan you beat in the butter quickly and vigorously to bind the sauce without cooking the butter (to my mind, definitely something to avoid). A tip: always use frozen cubes of butter, straight from the freezer. The coldness of the butter "shocks" the sauce into emulsifying, making it lighter and more airy. Serve immediately.

### CHOICE OF BUTTER

Always salted butter, which means reducing the quantity of salt in the dish accordingly. Other favorites are Jean-Yves' Espelette chili butter and raspberry-flavored butter.

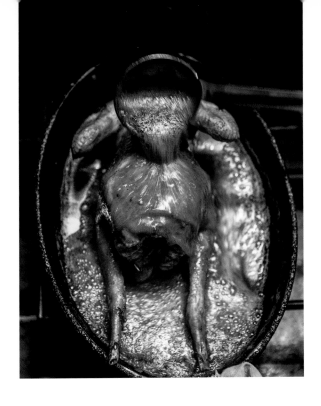

# Enriching

**BY LUC MOBIHAN,**
**LE SAINT-PLACIDE, ST. MALO**

## WHY ENRICH WITH BUTTER?

Quite simply, to add lusciousness and fragrance to cooking and patisserie. Melting butter in a pan and listening to it splutter and sizzle... Being careful not to burn it, remembering that butter is a fragile, natural thing. Watching for the moment when the butter turns from just melted to brown, rich with the promise of "lusciousness and fragrance." Nobody did it better than my grandparents when they cooked onions in butter to serve with a traditional black *far breton* and *kig ha farz*.

## USES

Enriching with butter tenderizes meat, makes it crisp and succulent. Drizzle melted butter over roast meat or fish *à la meunière* as they cook, then again at the end of cooking. Add a dollop of fresh butter to sautéed potatoes (taking care not to let it burn) and tuck some butter under the skin of chicken to bring out its fleshiness. Butter, plain or flavored with garlic, herbs or spices, works wonders with a bird. And for dessert? A glug of brown butter poured into a *far Breton* before cooking will not disappoint. Delicious!

## HOW IT'S DONE?

Melt the butter, whisking constantly, until it reaches a temperature of 140°-150°C (284°-302°F). Drizzle over food as it cooks and once cooking is finished.

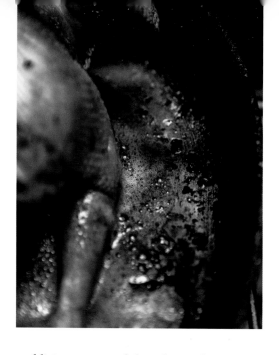

# Roasting

**BY THIERRY BRETON,
CHEZ MICHEL, CHEZ
CASIMIR AND LA POINTE
DU GROUIN, PARIS**

## WHO NEEDS CHEFS WHEN YOU HAVE ROASTS THAT SING?

Roasting is a delicate art. And never more so than when you're looking to make your roast sing. You want it crispy on the outside, tender on the inside. And that takes real mastery. Otherwise you are more likely to end up with something cooked to death on the outside and raw on the inside. So for large cuts of meat, resting time is essential. Roast beef for instance should be left to rest for half the cooking time before carving, turning it over at least twice. Ditto for poultry, except that you don't need to turn it over. Simply leave the bird to stand with breast uppermost so that none of the lovely juices escape. And roasting doesn't necessarily mean oven roast or spit roast. You can also roast in a skillet, modern-style, or over a wood fire as our ancestors did (known in French as *rôtir à la casse*, from the name of the utensil they used in the Ille-et-Vilaine department). In addition to meat, fish such as sole, turbot and salt cod (why not?) are ideal roasting candidates. Whatever the roast, always have a spoon at the ready and always keep your eye on the beast itself. Baste it constantly, drizzling the butter over the thickest parts to instill buttery flavor in the roast and ensure it cooks evenly. And talking of butter, always use semi-salted butter. It is less likely to burn (helpful if you're clumsy) and penetrates deep into the flesh, rather than just seasoning the skin. Which means more tastiness and less saltiness.

We chef's talk a lot about food "singing." Because we don't just look, feel and taste when we cook. We also listen. Put a slug of salted butter in a skillet, watch it melt, then listen to it sing as the water evaporates and the sizzling grows ever louder ... What you then roast in the butter is neither here nor there. It's the sound it makes that matters.

# Confire
## (slow cooking),

**BY ALAIN PASSARD,
CHEF AT L'ARPEGE,
PARIS**

I love slow-cooking vegetables such as
chicory in salted butter. Adding a touch
of seasoning at the beginning keeps them
looking fresh, locks in their subtle flavor
and, most important, preserves all of that
lovely crisp texture. Rather than drizzle
butter over my vegetables. I prefer to
turn them in the butter over a low flame,
always controlling the heat. Grilling is
another technique I use at the restaurant.
It draws out the fat in poultry, which I dot
with fresh butter at the end of cooking ...
For me salted butter brings back memories
of childhood ... My grandmother used to
spend hours at the stove slow-cooking her
vegetables. They were always very thinly
sliced, and soaked up the salted butter
as they cooked. She would toss them at
regular intervals to give them a lovely
golden color. Then serve them with a
spit-roasted leg of lamb or an oven-baked
chicken, surrounded by new potatoes –
slow-cooked in salted butter of course!
Delicious!

JEAN-YVES BORDIER'S

# EASIEST-EVER BREAD AND BUTTER RECIPE

Take the butter out of the refrigerator at least 15 minutes before use. The ideal serving temperature is about 18o°C (64.4o°F), which is a moderate room temperature.

Remove the outer layer from part of your stick of butter.

Cut off a small piece of butter using a non-serrated knife.

Place your piece of butter on the edge of a crusty slice of bread and for goodness' sake (literally) don't spread it. Butter is a noble food – you can't treat it like plastic wrap.

Bite gently into the bread and butter and feel the taste explode on your taste buds as the fat content in the butter yields up its complex bouquet.

Indulge in a moment of delectable, exquisite surrender!

Remember to put your butter back in the fridge. Butter is a fresh milk product and should be stored at 0-6°C (32-42.8°F), away from light, air and foreign odors. Keep it wrapped in its original packaging, parchment paper, plastic wrap or aluminum foil, or better still in a covered butter dish.

All you need now is some real French bread – and anyway you slice it, French bread doesn't come more traditional than Apollonia Poilâne's wonderful loaves.


Jean-Yves Bordier,

Wholly devoted to your bread and butter!

## BREAD
## AND BUTTER

**TEXT BY APOLLONIA POILANE**

**APOLLONIA POILANE**

Owner of La Maison Poilâne,
one of the greatest names
in French *boulangeries*.

Bread and butter come from the same source: the earth. The earth produces the grain that makes the flour, and the grass that makes the milk. Both are nourished by the same creative energies: the water and sun that turn the grain into grasses and the grasses into ears of corn.

Bread and butter are the ultimate expression of life. Earth, water, fire and air, the four primeval elements, joined forces to turn bread and butter into foods that bring us together.

Bread and butter are natural "companions" (meaning "the person who shares your bread", from the Latin *cum panem*). Disarmingly simple, but with delicious layers of flavors worthy of a gourmet delicacy – ask any French schoolchild. Bread and butter are made for enjoying around the breakfast table with *les copains* (friends, literally "sharers of bread"). What better than the scent of hot buttered toast to start the day, the melting butter fusing with the richness of the bread? Unless, of course, we go for an indulgence even wilder than my father, Lionel Poilâne's "bread sandwich". Not just two slices of fresh bread on either side of a slice of toast, but a slice of toast that is buttered on one side with sweet butter and on the other side with salted butter. Tender on the outside, crispy on the inside, a perfect melding of softness and substance.

Bread and butter are intimately linked and they create intimate links between those who eat them and those who make them. In France we talk of *gagne-pain*, in English-speaking countries it's "bread and butter". But for those of us who make bread and butter, it isn't just a job. It's a calling. A commitment to safeguard skills and a savoir-faire that date back thousands of years.

## SOME MEURSAULT
## FOR MY BUTTER

**TEXT BY ERIC BEAUMARD**

**ERIC BEAUMARD**

Chef Sommelier and Restaurant
Director of Le Cinq, the three
Michelin-starred restaurant of
the Hotel George V in Paris

Butter can often be the unexpected ally of wine! This issue came up one day when I was with a *vigneron* friend from Châteauneuf-du-Pape. With most white wines from southern France, you want to retain a certain degree of sharpness for the sake of balance. This is usually achieved by preventing the second or so-called malolactic fermentation (ML), which is a natural deacidification process that converts malic acid into creamier-tasting lactic acid. Suppressing this conversion preserves the wines' crisp acidity, making them the perfect foil for olive oil. Burgundy wines on the other hand are intentionally put through ML to enhance their suppleness and fullness, and balance the flavors. The white wines take on notes of vanilla, licorice, a buttery richness that flirts deliciously with the taste of butter itself. A good country loaf, some very good butter, a very good Burgundy – these are life's simple pleasures at their very best.

# The advantage of using butter in patisserie

**BY STEPHANE DENIS,**
**PATISSERIE-MAKER IN ST. MALO**

Use it cold, softened (*beurre pommade*) or melted ... butter plays on the texture of patisserie and helps to bring out the taste of the other ingredients. Cold butter is used in *sablage*, cutting the butter into the flour to make a friable, short-bread dough (*pâte sablée*). *Beurre pommade* beaten together with eggs and sugar helps to make cakes moist, light and fluffy. The air beaten into the butter helps patisseries to rise as they cook. Melted butter produces a cake batter with a fairly dense but dropping consistency that is ideal for pancakes and *financiers* (small sponge biscuit cakes).

## PUFF PASTRY

As butter melts it "waterproofs" the layers of dough, preventing the steam in the dough from escaping, which in turn pushes the layers apart. It is these alternating layers of dough and air that give puff pastry its light and flaky texture. Good puff pastry has several hundred layers of dough that rise in the course of cooking.

The trick is not letting the fat melt as you work the dough – you don't want to incorporate it into the dough, you want it to act as a barrier to the steam. So remember to chill the dough in between each round of rolling and folding.

Puff pastry can be divided into two types: classic puff pastry, where the butter is worked into the *détrempe* (base dough); and inverse puff pastry, where the *détrempe* is worked into the butter.

### CLASSIC PUFF PASTRY

Make a *détrempe* with fine wheat flour, salt and water then knead in the mixer bowl with a dough hook until a soft dough forms. Wrap in plastic wrap and refrigerate overnight. The next day, roll out the *détrempe* to form a square. Now work in "dry butter" (*beurre de tourage* or special puff pastry butter – which should be the same consistency as the dough.) Place the butter at an angle in the center of the *abaisse* (your pastry square) and fold the edges over the butter. Roll out the dough into a rectangle, fold into thirds and give it a quarter of a turn. Then roll and fold into thirds again and leave to rest in the fridge for 30 minutes.

Repeat twice, letting the dough rest between times.

Wrap the dough in plastic wrap and set aside in the fridge.

When time comes to use it, roll out the dough as required by the recipe, remembering to let it rest before cutting and also before cooking.

### INVERSE PUFF PASTRY

Incorporate the *détrempe* into the butter then proceed as for classic puff pastry. Inverse puff pastry is easier to work, rises a lot more in cooking and takes on a crispy but also melt-in-the-mouth texture.

## PÂTE SABLÉE
(SHORTBREAD DOUGH)

Use to make tarts and pies. Shortbread dough is made by a technique called "cutting in": working cold butter into flour and sugar so as to coat each grain of the dry ingredients. This keeps them separate as they bake, producing a crust with a crumbly texture.

Mix together the flour, butter, salt and raising agent, then cut in the butter using the flat whisk attachment on the mixer. Prepare an emulsion with egg yokes, sugar and a few vanilla seeds (scraped out of a vanilla pod that is split lengthways). Combine with the flour and butter to form a smooth dough. Set aside in the fridge before use.

## PÂTE BRISÉE
(SHORT PASTRY)

Use to make savory tarts. The recipe calls for softened butter that is not fully incorporated into the flour, producing pastry with a distinctively smooth and crisp texture. Mix together flour, butter and coarse salt in the mixer bowl using the flat beater. Add the egg yokes, mix again, then add the water. Now work everything together until the dough comes together and forms a ball, using the heel of your hand to distribute the fat evenly (known in French as *fraiser*). Don't overwork the dough or it will be too crumbly.

## GÂTEAU BRETON

A moist cake with a golden crust and a friable, crumbly texture similar to *palet breton*. Mix together flour and sugar, rub in some semi-salted butter then add egg yokes, being careful not to overwork the dough. Leave to rest for 24 hours. Brush with egg yoke then bake at 160°C (320°F) for 45 minutes.

# RECIPES

# Black radish nibbles with different butters

Preparation time
**15 minutes**

**Serves 4**

1 black radish of about 300 g (½ lb)

50 g (⅓ cup) raspberry butter

50 g (⅓ cup) lemon-olive oil butter

50 g (⅓ cup) curry butter

50 g (⅓ cup) yuzu butter

50 g (⅓ cup) herbal butter and Sishuan pepper

50 g (2 ½ cups) New Zealand spinach leaves

Wash the radish thoroughly under running water with a brush, then cut into thin slices.

Spread one of the butters on a slice of radish, cover with another slice and cut the sandwich in half. Repeat the process with the other slices, using the five butters alternately.

Offer these little veggie sandwiches as nibbles with an aperitif, accompanied by New Zealand spinach leaves.

# Salmon gravlax with crunchy bread and butter

**Make 14 hr ahead**

Preparation time
**30 minutes**

Cooking time
**15 minutes**

**Serves 4**

For the salmon gravlax:

50 g (½ cup) sugar

100 g (1 cup) coarse grey salt

10 g (1 tsp) pepper

5 g (½ tsp) Jamaican pepper

5 g (nearly a ¼ cup) fennel flower

320 g (9 ½ oz) salmon

3 cl (2 tbsp) cider vinegar

1 organic lemon

For the vegetable pickles :

½ bunch red radishes

1 carrot

1 Roscoff (red) onion

50 cl (2 cups) cider vinegar

Honey

For the crunchy canapés:

2 thin baguettes

50 g (⅓ cup) Espelette chili butter

50 g (⅓ cup) seaweed butter

50 g (⅓ cup) yuzu butter

½ bunch coriander

**PREPARATION**

Prepare the salmon gravlax. The day before, mix the sugar, coarse salt, and crushed spices and rub into the salmon where the skin was removed. Chill for 8 – 10 hours.

**THE PICKLES**

Quarter the radishes, peel the carrots, remove the cores with an apple corer and slice thinly with the mandolin. Chop the onion. Boil each vegetable separately in cider vinegar, correcting the acidity with a little honey if needed.

**THE SALMON**

Remove the dry marinade from the fish and rinse it with cider vinegar. Sprinkle grated lemon zest over the salmon and cut it into 1.5 cm (¾ in) cubes.

**PRESENTATION**

Thinly slice the baguette and spread each slice with a different butter. Add a salmon cube and the pickles: the carrot with the Espelette chili butter, the onion with the seaweed butter and the radishes with the yuzu butter. Decorate with a coriander leaf.

# Mountain ham fingers
# with Espelette chili butter

Preparation time
**10 minutes**

**Serves 4**

50 g (⅓ cup) Espelette chili butter

20 g (⅔ cup) Sorrel shoots

4 slices bread

4 slices mountain ham

In a bowl, combine the Espelette chili butter with some of the sorrel shoots cut with scissors (keep some whole for decoration).

Toast the bread and cut the slices into strips. Butter generously and then top with the ham also cut into strips, and the remaining sorrel shoots.

These snacks for apéritif can be accompanied by a white wine such as a Terre de Pierre from domaine Luneau-Papin, or a red wine such as a Statera from the domaine de Bellevue (Jérôme Bretaudeau).

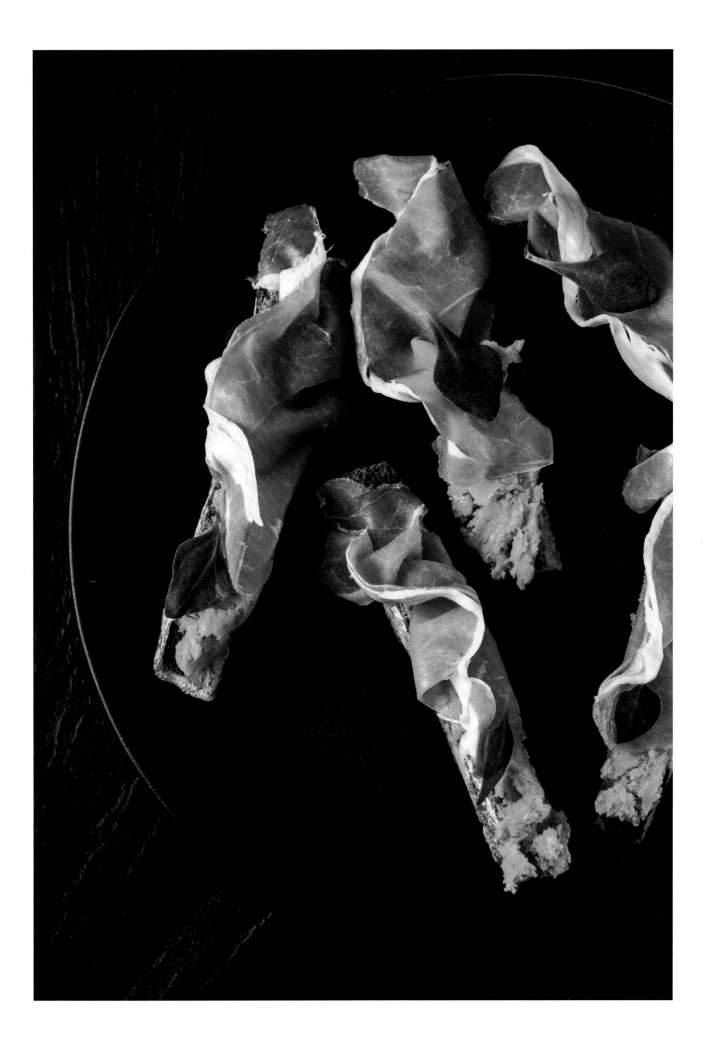

# Duck fillet bouchées, raspberry butter

Preparation time
**40 minutes**

Cooking time
**25 minutes**

**Serves 4**

200 g (7 ½ oz) small new potatoes

30 g (¼ cup) semi-salted butter

2 duck fillets

100 g (⅔ cup) raspberry butter

2 shallots

50 cl (2 cups) white wine

1 bunch dill

**PREPARATION**

Cook the unpeeled, thoroughly washed new potatoes in the salted butter over gentle heat in a covered pot.

**THE DUCK FILLETS**

Grill or sauté the duck fillets for about 15 minutes until hot yet rare, and leave to rest. Then slice thinly and leave aside between two warm plates on a corner of the hob.

**THE SHALLOTS**

While the meat is cooking, cut the raspberry butter into cubes and finely chop the shallots. Reduce the chopped shallots in the white wine in a small saucepan. When the equivalent of a tablespoon of liquid remains, pour it into a double saucepan and gradually whip in the butter cubes.

**PRESENTATION**

Wrap each potato in a slice of duck fillet and secure with a toothpick. Decorate with the dill and serve with the raspberry butter.

# Olive, pepper, butter and herb open sandwiches

Preparation time
**15 minutes**

Cooking time
**10 minutes**

**Serves 4**

1 red pepper

100 g (⅔ cup) green olives

100 g (⅔ cup) black olives

½ bunch basil

1 organic lime

8 thick slices of farmhouse bread

50 g (⅓ cup) fennel butter

50 g (⅓ cup) lemon-olive oil butter

**THE PEPPER**

Grill the pepper on a fork, turning it directly over a hot flame, then wrap it in greaseproof paper to cool. Once cool, peel and cut it into small cubes.

**THE OLIVES**

Pit the green and black olives and crush them with a knife, keeping the colors separate. Mix the crushed green olives with the chopped basil, and the crushed black olives with the lime zest.

**PRESENTATION**

Butter 4 slices of bread with fennel butter and top with the black olive mixture. Butter the other four slices with the lemon-olive oil butter and top with the green olive mixture.

Scatter the pepper cubes over all the slices and serve with apéritifs.

# Curry butter guacamole dip with raw vegetables

Preparation time
**15 minutes**

**Serves 4**

500 g (3 ½ cups) carrots

300 g (3 cups) small endives

1 small cauliflower

1 bunch red radishes

100 g (⅔ cup) curry butter

2 ripe avocadoes

1 lime

Salt

Cut the carrots and endives into sticks, the cauliflower into florets on toothpicks, and the radishes into quarters. Leave to chill on a large serving plate.

Whizz the curry butter with the avocado flesh and season with salt and the juice of the lime.

This dish can be accompanied by vegetable pickles and other marinated vegetables (peppers, olives) for light aperitif snacks.

# Filo pastry tart with long turnips and raspberry butter

Preparation time
**1 hour**

Cooking time
**45 minutes**

**Serves 4**

125 g (nearly 1 cup) raspberry butter

3 sheets filo pastry

10 cl (nearly ½ cup) olive oil

1 organic lemon

1 Roscoff (red) onion

1 kg (2 lb, 10 cups) long turnips

1 bunch chervil

Salt

**PREPARATION**

Place the raspberry butter in the freezer.

**FILO PASTRY TARTLETS**

Preheat the oven to 160°C (320°F, th. 5-6). Spread the first sheet of filo pastry on a clean board. Oil it with a brush, scatter it with a little lemon zest and salt slightly. Lay a second sheet on the first one and repeat the process with this and the third sheet, then fold the pastry in two, edge to edge. Cut out 4 discs 10 cm (4 in.) in diameter. Bake at 160°C (320°F) for 12 minutes. Once cooked, set aside on kitchen paper.

**THE ONION**

Thinly slice the onion, and cook it gently in a covered saucepan with the lemon juice and some salt until stewed.

Take out the raspberry butter. Cut half into thin curls and store in the freezer on a cling filmed plate. Cut the remaining butter into small cubes.

**THE TURNIPS**

Preheat the oven to 180°C (360°F, th. 6). Cut the turnips into thin, regular slices with the mandolin. Line four 10 cm (4 in) tartlet tins with greaseproof paper. Fill with turnip slices. Season, scatter with small cubes of butter, cover with greaseproof paper and bake for 20 minutes at 180°C (360°F).

**PRESENTATION**

Once out of the oven, remove the greaseproof paper covering the turnips and replace it with the stewed onion. Top with the filo pastry discs and then turn over to unmould the turnips. Cover with curls of raspberry butter and reheat the tartlets at 180°C (360°F) for ten minutes. Decorate with sprigs of chervil.

# Winkle canapés
# with tajine butter

Preparation time
**30 minutes**

Cooking time
**10 minutes**

**Serves 4**

1 kg (2 lb) winkles

30 g (1 tblsp) coarse grey salt

1 bouquet garni (thyme, laurel, rosemary)

8 slices of farmhouse bread

100 g (⅔ cup) tajine butter

2 wild dill flowers

1 organic lemon

Freshly ground white pepper

**THE WINKLES**

Mix the coarse salt in 1 litre (2 pints) cold water and pour in the winkles, adding the bouquet garni and 20 rotations of the peppermill. Bring to the boil and then turn off the heat. Put the winkles in the cooking water in a cool place ten minutes later. Once the winkles are cold, shell them and put aside to chill.

**PRESENTATION**

Toast the bread, add a thick layer of tajine butter and top with the winkles and dill flowers. Sprinkle with grated lemon zest.

# Old fashioned sardines and butter

*For many Bretons, this is a childhood memory : canned sardines could be found in every family storecupboard.*

Preparation time
**5 minutes**

**Serves 4**

1 can of plain sardines (no oil)

50 g (⅓ cup) semi-salted butter

1 Roscoff (red) onion

1 bunch chervil

½ bunch dill

100 g (5 cups) rocket

2 tbsp cider vinegar

Slices of farmhouse bread

**PREPARATION**

Drain the sardines. Empty onto a plate and mash into the semi-salted butter. Peel the onion and chop it, the chervil and the dill finely. Mix everything together and add a dash of vinegar.

**PRESENTATION**

Cut slices of farmhouse bread and spread them with the preparation. Decorate with rocket leaves.

# Zucchini, chanterelles and basil foam

Preparation time
**30 minutes**

Cooking time
**40 minutes**

**Serves 4**

½ cucumber

1 organic lime

50 g (⅓ cup) roasted buckwheat seeds (kasha), crushed

100 g (⅔ cup) salted butter

1 egg

2 small yellow zucchini (300 g, 2 ½ cups)

2 small green zucchini (300 g, 2 ½ cups)

20 g (¼ cup) stick almonds

1 bunch basil

50 cl (2 cups) chicken stock

200 g (3⅓ cups) chanterelles

1 stick rhubarb

Salt

**PREPARATION**

Slice the ½ cucumber and marinate it with salt and the lime zest.

**THE BUCKWHEAT DOUGH**

Preheat the oven to 180°C (360°F, th. 6). In a saucepan, sauté the buckwheat seeds with 20g (⅛ cup) butter. Once slightly browned add 15 cl (½ cup) water and some salt. Cover, and simmer gently for 25 minutes, stirring regularly. Once cooled, combine with the egg. Roll out this buckwheat dough in a square 12cm (5 in) a side, and place on a cooking tray. Bake at 180°C (360°F) for 7 minutes. Cut four strips in the cooked square, then sauté them and put aside.

**THE ZUCCHINI**

Preheat the oven to 200°C (390°F, th. 6-7). Cut thin lengthwise slices in the zucchini using a mandolin, then salt them. Lay 20 zucchini slices flat on a buttered tray and bake for five minutes at 200°C (390°F). Then roll the zucchini slices and skewer each with an almond stick. Place the rolls on a tray in a warm oven.

**THE EMULSION**

In a food mixer, gradually pour the hot chicken stock over the whizzing basil leaves and add 50 g (¼ cup) butter cubes and a dash of lime juice, then sieve the foam.

**THE CHANTERELLES**

At the last minute, fry the chanterelles in a little butter.

**PRESENTATION**

Present the zucchini rolls and the chanterelles on the buckwheat strips, sprinkle with slivers of rhubarb and the marinated cucumber, and finish with the basil foam.

# Gougères and their hazelnut butter crunch

Preparation time
**25 minutes**

Cooking time
**25 minutes**

**Pour 30 pièces**

For the crunch:

60 g (nearly ½ cup) semi-salted butter

60 g (¾ cup) ground hazelnuts

40 g (⅓ cup) all-purpose flour

30 g (¼ cup) sesame flour

For the gougères:

250 ml (1 cup) water

75 g (½ cup) salted butter

150 g (1 ¼ cups) all-purpose flour

4 eggs

150 g (1⅓ cups) grated swiss cheese

**THE CRUNCH**

In a bowl, combine the softened butter, the ground hazelnuts, the all-purpose flour and the sesame flour. Roll out very thinly on greaseproof paper laid on a baking tray. Chill in the freezer.

**THE GOUGÈRES**

Boil the water in a saucepan with the butter. Off the flame, add in the flour and gradually stir the mixture with a spatula until dry and coming off the sides of the saucepan. Cool and then add the eggs one by one, finishing with the grated cheese. Place the mixture in a pastry bag and squeeze out 30 identical balls onto a baking tray covered in greaseproof paper.

**ASSEMBLY**

Preheat the oven to 180°C (360°F, th. 6). Take the crunch dough out of the freezer and cut out 30 discs 4cm (1 ½ in) in diameter. Place one on each gougère before baking at 180°C (360°F) for 25 minutes. Serve lukewarm.

# Jacknife (razor) clams in wild fennel butter

**Preparation time**
**40 minutes**

**Cooking time**
**15 minutes**

**Serves 4**

4 large jacknife (razor) clams

1 x 150 g (5 oz) squash

50 g (⅓ cup) Sichuan pepper butter

1 Menton lemon (or mildly acidic lemon)

100 g (⅔ cup) yuzu butter

½ bunch chives

Wild fennel flowers

### THE JACKNIFE (RAZOR) CLAMS

Clean the jacknife (razor) clams thoroughly in seawater and then open them by sliding a blade between the shell and the flesh. Remove the black pocket and intestines and then replace the flesh in one half of the shell. Chill.

### THE SQUASH

Cut the squash into 16 narrow pieces, leaving the skin. Sauté in a covered pan with the Sichuan pepper butter. Once cooked, add the Menton lemon zest.

### COOKING

Pre-heat the oven to 180°C (360°F, th. 6). Place the clams in an oven dish, scatter yuzu butter curls over them and bake for about 12 minutes at 180°C (360°F). Baste regularly with the butter (which gently cooks the clam).

### PRESENTATION

Place the squash pieces and the jacknife (razor) clams on hot plates. Garnish with chopped chives and fennel flowers. Finally, drizzle with a little lemon juice.

# Braised chicory,
# pear and mead butter

Preparation time
**20 minutes**

Cooking time
**25 minutes**

**Serves 4**

125 g (nearly ¾ cup) semi-salted butter

20 cl (¾ cup) mead

1 organic orange

4 x organic chicory

1 comice pear depending on size

1 lid seal (mix 250 g (2 cups) flour with 15cl (½ cup) water to form a paste)

½ bunch sorrel

Fleur de sel

**PREPARATION**

In a bowl, mix the softened butter, the mead and the zest of the orange, then place in the freezer.

**THE CHICORY AND THE PEAR**

Pre-heat the oven to 180°C (360°F, th. 6). Cut the pear in half and remove core. Place each half face down on the cutting board and cut 16 thin slices from tail to end. Cut the chicory in half lengthwise and insert four slices of pear between the leaves of each, then place face down in a lidded oven dish. Cover with curls of the butter cut with the peeling knife and seal the lid with the flour paste. Bake for 25 minutes at 180°C (360°F).

**PRESENTATION**

If the chicory seem a little pale on leaving the oven, caramelize them lightly in the frying pan over a gentle heat, cut side down, and then season with the fleur de sel and present on hot plates accompanied by sorrel leaves and cooking jus.

# Salsify Tagliatelli with mussels and tajine butter

Preparation time
**20 minutes**

Cooking time
**15 minutes**

**Serves 4**

1 kg (7 ½ cups, 2 ¼ lb) salsify

1 organic lemon

1 Roscoff (pink) onion

500 g (1 lb) mussels

50 cl (2 cups) yellow wine

100 g (⅔ cup) tajine butter

200 g (6⅔ cups) New Zealand spinach

### PREPARATION

Peel the salsify wearing gloves, then cover with water and lemon juice to prevent blackening. Slice thinly lengthwise with the mandolin, and replace these salsify tagliatelli in the lemon water.

### THE MUSSELS

Thinly slice the Roscoff onion and sweat it in the butter. Clean the mussels, then open them over a hot flame in a covered pan with the onion and the yellow wine for about 5 minutes. Shell most of the mussels but keep a few with shells for decoration. Strain the cooking liquid and put aside.

### THE SALSIFY

Before serving, sauté the salsify tagliatelli with half the tajine butter until slightly browned, then remove when still slightly crunchy and keep warm.

In the same sauté pan, whip together the mussel cooking liquid and the remaining butter until thick. Now add in the tagliatelli, the New Zealand spinach leaves and the mussels. Serve in deep dishes, sprinkled with lemon zest to add zing.

# Mushrooms in foaming walnut and tarragon butter

Preparation time
**20 minutes**

Cooking time
**15 minutes**

**Serves 4**

1 kg (2 ¼ lb) small brown mushrooms

2 finely chopped shallots

200 g (1⅓ cups) semi-salted butter

½ bunch tarragon

100 g (1 ¼ cups) crushed walnuts

30 g (¼ cup) dry breadcrumbs

**MUSHROOMS**

Preheat the oven to 180°C (360°F, th. 6). Wash and trim the tails from the mushrooms. Place the heads on the flat sides in an earthenware dish. Chop the tails into cubes and fry in 50g (⅓ cup) butter in a saucepan with the shallots. Stuff the heads with this mixture and bake at 180°C (360°F, th. 6) for 15 minutes.

**THE FOAMING BUTTER**

Meanwhile, strip and crush the tarragon, then leave aside. Heat the crushed walnuts in the remaining butter, shaking the pan in a circular movement to ensure the butter is always moving and foamy – this will enable the walnuts to roast gently and infuse the butter. Then sprinkle the breadcrumbs over the butter while continuing to shake the pan (this densifies the mixture). Off the flame, mix in the tarragon, while still shaking.

**PRESENTATION**

Remove the mushroom heads from the oven and with a teaspoon, fill each with the foaming butter. Present immediately on hot plates.

# Bread crunchy, vanilla butter and cocoa nibs

Preparation time
**10 minutes**

Cooking time
**10 minutes**

**Serves 4**

50 g (½ cup) cocoa nibs

150 g (¾ cup) confectioner's sugar

8 slices farmhouse bread

100 g (⅔ cup) vanilla butter

**PREPARATION**

Roast the cocoa nibs in a frying pan, stirring regularly with a spatula, then gradually sprinkle in the sugar. It will caramelize around the cocoa nibs. Repeat the operation until the sugar has finished, then spread to cool on greaseproof paper.

Toast the farmhouse bread slices then top with curls of vanilla butter. Sprinkle with the caramelized cocoa nibs.

These toasts can be served with coffee or tea.

# Leeks in a clay shell with lemon-olive oil butter

Preparation time
**15 minutes**

Cooking time
**40 minutes**

**Serves 4**

 4 large fresh leeks

1 kg (2¼ lbs) clay

50 g (½ cups) lemon olive-oil butter

Fleur de sel

**THE LEEKS**

Preheat the oven to 180°C (360°F, th. 6). Strip off the outer leaves of the leeks and discard. Wash the leeks carefully, rubbing the roots. Roll out the clay on two sheets of greaseproof paper with a rolling pin, to a thickness of 0.5 cm (¼ in). Cut the sheets in half lengthwise and wrap them around the leeks (clean side inwards). Cut the remaining clay into strips and tie around each leek packet, ensuring that the shell is firmly sealed by wetting and squeezing the join with your fingers.

Bake at 180°C (360°F) on a baking tray for 40 minutes and then remove and leave to rest for 15 minutes.

**PRESENTATION**

To serve, present the clay shells to your guests and break them with a sharp hammer blow, then open and discard the shells and paper. Split each leek with a knife and insert lumps of the butter. Finish by sprinkling with fleur de sel.

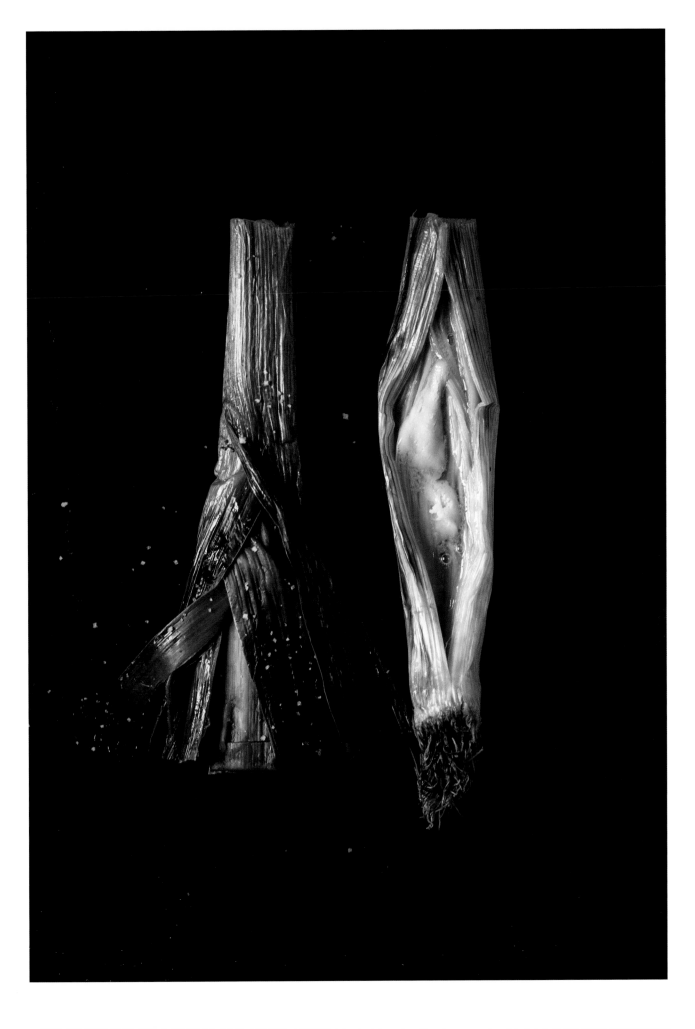

# Egg parfait, artichoke and smoked salt butter

Preparation time
**1 hour**

Cooking time
**1 hour**

**Serves 4**

4 organic free range eggs

4 artichokes

1 organic lime

10 cl (½ cup) chicken stock

1 l (4 cups) groundnut oil

100 g (⅔ cup) smoked salt butter

Salt

**THE EGGS**

Cook the eggs in a double saucepan or in a steam oven at 63°C (145°F) for 1 hour.

**THE ARTICHOKE**

Remove the artichoke leaves, trim to the base and remove the hairs from the centre, then rub the surface with the halved lime. Cut two of the artichoke hearts into cubes and simmer them in the chicken stock in a covered saucepan for 20 minutes. Once cooked, drain them but keep the remaining stock in the saucepan. Rub the flesh through a sieve to obtain a smooth purée. Thinly slice the remaining artichoke hearts with a mandolin and deep fry them in a sauteuse at 150°C (300°F) for a few minutes (taking care that the crisps do not brown too much, otherwise they are bitter and inedible). Drain on kitchen paper then dust with salt. Whip the remaining stock into a foam with the smoked butter.

**PRESENTATION**

When ready to serve, use a pastry bag to form circles of hot artichoke purée in heated shallow dishes, then break one egg into each circle. Add the artichoke crisps and the smoked salt butter foam.

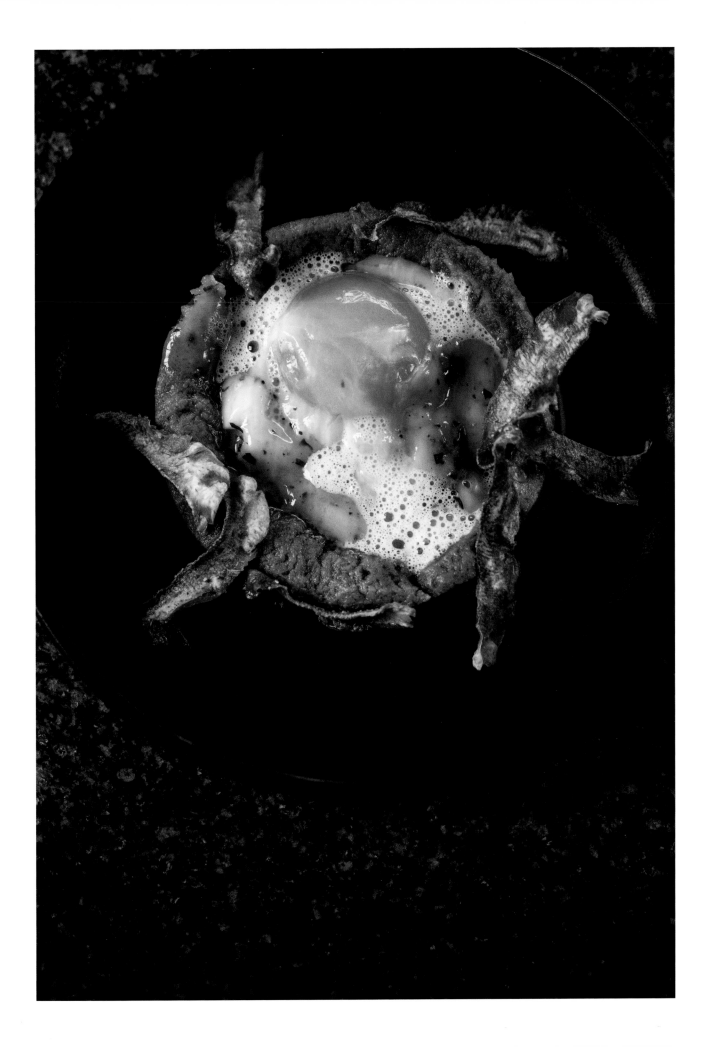

# Porcini tartlets with rocket and smoked salt butter

Preparation time
**30 minutes**

Cooking time
**40 minutes**

**Serves 4**

For the pastry shell:

1 finely chopped shallot

50 g (⅓ cup) smoked salt butter

80 g (⅔ cup) roasted buckwheat (kasha) seeds

15 cl (½ cup) chicken stock

3 g (½ tsp) fresh grated ginger

30 g (1 oz) beaten egg (1 egg white)

10 g (½ tbsp) flat parsley leaves

Salt

For the mushrooms:

200 g (2 cups) baby porcini

Sunflower oil

Deglazing jus:

100 g (⅓ cup) smoked salt butter

40 cl (1 ½ cups) chicken stock

**TARTLET SHELL**

Sweat the shallot in a small saucepan with the smoked butter, then add in the buckwheat seeds, chicken stock, grated ginger and a pinch of salt. Cover and cook over a gentle flame for about 30 minutes.

Preheat the oven to 180°C (360°F, th. 6). Once the seeds are cooked and cooled, mix the egg and minced parsley into the pastry and roll it out into a 14cm (5 ½ in) square on greaseproof paper placed on a baking tray. Bake for 10 minutes at 180°C (360°F). Once it has cooled, cut it into four strips.

**THE MUSHROOMS**

Clean with a damp cloth and cut into 1cm (¼ in) slices. Sauté each side in the sunflower oil over a hot flame then leave aside on warmed plates.

**PRESENTATION**

Put eight curls of smoked butter on a clingfilmed plate in the freezer.

Prepare the jus. Whip the chicken stock (which has deglazed the mushroom frying pan) with the remaining smoked butter in a saucepan.

Slightly brown the pastry strips in an oiled pan. Place the porcini on each strip, and scatter with the curls of smoked salt butter. Present the porcini tartlets on a bed of rocket glazed with walnut oil, and serve with the jus.

# Brussels sprouts, turmeric butter and sea urchins

Preparation time
**20 minutes**

Cooking time
**20 minutes**

**Serves 4**

5 g (⅛ cup) fresh turmeric root, grated

2 organic lemons

200 g (1⅓ cup) semi-salted butter

200 g (2 ¼ cups) Brussels sprouts

4 fresh sea urchins (or 20 roes)

3 egg yolks

1 sharp apple

Salt

Baking soda

**PREPARATION**

On the day before, peel the fresh curcuma root. Grate it onto the butter and then add the lemon zests before mixing. Chill the flavoured butter covered with clingfilm to protect it from the air.

**THE BRUSSELS SPROUTS**

The next day, trim the Brussels sprouts keeping the 20 green outer leaves (these will serve as little shells for the sauce on presentation). Cut the sprouts in half and cook for 10 minutes in boiling salted water with a pinch of baking soda. Once cooked, plunge into iced water to stop the cooking and then place aside at room temperature. Now repeat the process with the outer leaves for about five minutes so that they are still crunchy. Once they are drained, place sea urchin roe in each little shell.

**THE EMULSION**

Remove the chilled butter from the fridge and cut into cubes. Whip the egg yolks with two tbsp water in a double saucepan (heating gently to foam it like a sabayon) and gradually incorporate the cold butter cubes to whip up a sauce like a hollandaise. Season with salt and the remaining lemon juice.

**PRESENTATION**

Present the Brussels sprouts reheated in the oven on hot plates, then add the shells with sea urchin roe and pour into each a teaspoonful of sauce. Decorate with apple sticks.

# Clams stuffed with a selection of butters

Preparation time
**15 minutes**

Cooking time
**10 minutes**

Serves 4

30 g (1 tbsp) coarse sea salt

48 large clams

100 g (⅔ cup) yuzu butter

20 g (nearly ¼ cup) ground almonds

100 g (⅔ cup) Espelette chili butter

20 g (nearly ¼ cup) ground hazelnuts

100 g (⅔ cup) garlic and parsley butter

20 g (nearly ¼ cup) breadcrumbs

**PREPARATION**

The day before, prepare 2 litres of cold water, adding the sea salt.

The next day, wash the clams in water several times and then pour them into the prepared cold salted water to disgorge their sand.

**THE SELECTION OF BUTTERS**

Using a fork, mash up the yuzu butter with the ground almonds, then the Espelette chili butter with the ground hazelnuts, and finally the garlic and parsley butter with the breadcrumbs. Spread each butter very thinly on clingfilmed trays, and place in the freezer.

**THE CLAMS**

Drain the clams, allow the water to settle and then drain off the top into a saucepan to boil. Drop 10 clams at a time into the boiling water and remove to a stainless steel bowl as soon as the first one opens. Remove one half of the shell and cut the muscle holding the clam in the other half.

**PRESENTATION**

Using a cookie cutter, make discs in the butters. Top each clam with a disc, then put them all into an oven tray. Grill for a few minutes to complete the cooking.

# Soft-boiled egg
# and soldiers
# with vanilla butter

Preparation time
**10 minutes**

Cooking time
**5 minutes**

**Serves 4**

4 organic free-range eggs at room temperature

4 thin baguettes cut into soldiers

100 g (⅔ cup) vanilla butter

Fleur de sel

**PREPARATION**

Boil the eggs for 5-6 minutes.

Meanwhile, butter the toasted baguettes with the vanilla butter. If wished, lightly salt them with a little fleur de sel.

Simple comfort food for brunching!

# Warm oyster, buckwheat butter and lime

Preparation time
**10 minutes**

Cooking time
**15 minutes**

**Serves 4**

4 large flat oysters

80 g (½ cup) buckwheat butter

1 organic lime

Dill sprigs

### PREPARATION

Cover a large flat plate with tightly stretched clingfilm and place in the freezer. Cut 40 curls of buckwheat butter with a peeling knife and place them on the filmed plate (if the butter softens too quickly, return it to the freezer and repeat the process). Leave aside in the freezer.

### THE OYSTERS

Preheat the oven to 200°C (390°F, th.6-7). Open the oysters, pour off the water and cut the muscle. Bake for 10-12 minutes at 200°C (390°F). Make sure the oyster does not become leathery, just warm.

### PRESENTATION

Remove the oysters from the oven and top with the buckwheat butter curls, the grated lime zest and the dill sprigs. Eat immediately.

# Celery baked in salt,
# served with smoked salt butter

Preparation time
**20 minutes**

Cooking time
**1 hour**

**Serves 4**

250 g (1 ⅔ cups) smoked salt butter

1 fresh celeriac about 1.2 kg (2 ½ lb)

For the salt crust:

2 egg whites (60 g, 2 oz)

3 kg (6 ½ lbs) coarse sea salt (Guérande)

**PREPARATION**

Cover a large flat plate with clingfilm and place in the freezer.
Using a peeling knife, prepare 40 curls of smoked salt butter, and place
on the clingfilmed plate (if the butter softens too quickly, put it back in
the freezer and repeat the process). Put aside in the freezer.

**THE CELERIAC**

Preheat the oven to 200°C (390°F, th. 6-7). Wash the celeriac with a brush
under running water to remove all traces of earth. Make a cylinder about
3 cm (1 ½ in) wider than the diameter of the celeriac out of greaseproof
paper. Staple the cylinder to keep its shape.

**THE SALT CRUST**

In a round metal bowl, mix the egg whites into the coarse salt with your
hands. Place the greaseproof paper cylinder upright on an oven tray and
fill the bottom with a little of the salt mixture. Slide in the celeriac and then
fill up the sides and top of the tube around the celeriac with the rest of the
salt. The celeriac must be completely covered. Bake at 200°C (390°F) for
one hour.

**PRESENTATION**

Remove the celeriac from the oven, and leave at room temperature for
about ten minutes before presenting it at table. Break the salt crust with
the spine of a large knife and cut it into 8 pieces. Place them on hot plates
and top with smoked salt curls.

# Scallops in their shells with parsley root butter

Preparation time
**30 minutes**

Cooking time
**15 minutes**

**Serves 4**

50 g (⅓ cup) semi-salted butter

200 g (1 ½ cups) parsley root

1 organic lime

50 g (1 cup) stripped flat parsley

10 g (1 tsp) fresh horseradish

4 large scallops (Saint-Brieuc if possible)

Coarse salt

Sunflower oil

**PREPARATION**

Cut the butter into small 5 mm (⅛ in) cubes. Place on a clingfilmed plate in the freezer (the film stretched over it means the butter does not stick to the plate).

**THE PARSLEY ROOTS**

Peel the parsley roots. Cut into about 20 thin slices with a mandolin. Fry them in oil at 140°C (284°F) in a deep pan over a hot flame for a few minutes, then salt them and leave to dry on kitchen paper. Cut the remaining roots into cubes, and cook in a little water in a covered pan. Once they are cooked, mix to a smooth purée and add the lime zest.

**FLAT PARSLEY BUTTER**

Process the flat parsley leaves in a food mixer, regularly turning them back into the blade with a spatula, and then add the frozen butter lumps. These will pulverize the parsley as if they were little pebbles, thus bringing out the chlorophyll and turning the butter green. Once the butter is well mixed, correct the acidity with the lime juice and add in the freshly grated horseradish. Thinly spread the flavoured butter on a clingfilmed tray and place in the freezer.

**THE SCALLOPS**

Preheat the oven to 180°C (360°F, th. 6). Take out the butter and cut out rounds the same size as the scallops. Oil the scallop shells, then top the scallops with the butter rounds and bake for 4 minutes at 180°C (360°F) (the butter will be just melted and the scallops warm and half-cooked).

**PRESENTATION**

Take the scallops out of the oven and place each on a bed of coarse salt in a plate. To one side, add the parsley root puree and crisps.

# Red mullet, baked fennel and dill butter

Preparation time
**1 hour**

Cooking time
**40 minutes**

**Serves 4**

200 g (1⅓ cup) semi-salted butter

2 x 200 g (7 oz) red mullets

1 bunch dill

1 fennel root

1 lid seal (mix 250g (2 cups) flour with 15cl (½ cup) water to form a paste)

1 organic bergamot (or organic grapefruit)

Olive oil

**PREPARATION**

Cover a plate with tightly stretched cling film. Make 1 cm (¼ in) cubes with the butter, place on the filmed plate and freeze.

**THE MULLETS**

Fillet the mullets and then remove the inside bones with tweezers. Chill the fillets under a damp cloth.

**THE DILL BUTTER**

Shred the dill and place in the mixer with the butter cubes. Whizz until a smooth green preparation is obtained. Set half the dill butter aside and thinly spread the other half on a filmed plate in four squares 10cm (4 in) a side. Chill the plate.

**THE FENNEL**

Preheat the oven to 180°C (360°F, th. 6). Slice the fennel root into four slices 1.5 cm (¾ inch) thick. Place them flat in a lidded pan with the rest of the dill butter and seal the lid with the flour paste. Bake for 30 min at 180°C (360°F).

**PRESENTATION**

Place the squares of dill butter on the cooked fennel slices and re-heat them in the oven at 180°C (360°F, th. 6) for five minutes so that the melting butter coats the fennel, then cook the mullet fillets lightly brushed with olive oil in an oven dish for 6 minutes at 180°C (360°F, th. 6). Place the mullet fillets on the fennel slices, then sprinkle with grated bergamot.

Tip: To make a strongly colored and flavored herb butter, use hard butter which will crush the herbs as if it were gravel, due to the force of the mixer blade. The herb juice will thus blend into the butter and froth it.

# Confit of cod in seaweed butter and pickles

Preparation time
**40 minutes**

Cooking time
**25 minutes**

**Serves 4**

4 x 150 g (4oz) portions of line caught cod

50 cl (2 cups) cider vinegar

3 leaves sage

2 new carrots

10 red radishes

20 g (1 ½ tbsp) honey

250 g (1 ⅔ cups) seaweed butter

20 g (1 ½ tbsp) capers

½ bunch washed watercress

Salt

**PREPARATION**

In the morning, salt the fish lightly with powdered salt on all surfaces and chill on a cloth in the fridge.

**THE PICKLES**

In a saucepan combine 25 cl (1 cup) of cider vinegar and the sage leaves. Salt to taste and bring to the boil. Peel the carrots, remove the cores with an apple corer and slice thinly with the mandolin. Drop into the boiling cider vinegar and leave to cool at room temperature.

In another saucepan, pour the remaining cider vinegar. Salt, sweeten with the honey and bring to the boil. Wash and quarter the radishes and drop into the boiling vinegar. Leave to cool at room temperature.

**THE COD**

Preheat the oven to 160°C (320°F, th. 5-6). Twenty minutes before serving, slice the seaweed butter. Rinse the fish pieces under a trickle of water and dry, then place them in an earthenware dish with the butter slices on top. Bake for 15 minutes at 160°C (320°F, th. 5-6) taking care to remove the fish every 3 minutes and baste it with the melted butter on every surface.

**PRESENTATION**

When the fish begins to flake and become opaque at the edges, remove to hot plates. Decorate with the pickles (carrots, radish and capers) and watercress. Make a jus with the cooking butter, rectified with the radish vinegar.

# Braised cardoons, Espelette chili butter and fried onions

Preparation time
**30 minutes**

Cooking time
**1 hour 45**

**Serves 4**

150 g (1 cup) Espelette chili butter

1 organic lemon

1 bunch cardoons

4 Roscoff (mild red) onions

1 l (1 quart) chicken stock

1 bouquet garni (thyme, laurel, rosemary)

½ bunch flat parsley

10 cl (½ cup) sunflower oil

50 g (½ cup) Parmesan shavings

3 sprigs parsley

**PREPARATION**

Stretch clingfilm over a large flat plate and place in the freezer.
Using a peeling knife, pare off 40 curls of Espelette chili butter, placing them on the filmed plate (if the butter softens too quickly, replace it in the freezer and repeat the process). Leave aside in the freezer on the plate.

Remove the lemon zest with a peeling knife.

**THE CARDOONS**

Clean the cardoons with a brush under running water to remove the thin white outer skin. Cut into 10cm (4 in) lengths, and place in water with lemon juice to avoid blackening.

Peel the onions and remove the 3 outer skins. Finely chop these skins into the simmering chicken stock over a gentle flame then add the bouquet garni and the lemon zests (do not salt the stock, the slightly bitter taste of the cardoons would accentuate the saltiness). Simmer the cardoons in this stock in a covered pot for 1 ½ hours.

The cardoons are ready when they are soft when tested with a sharp knife point. Drain (keeping the stock) and gently sauté them for a good 10 minutes, in the rest of the Espelette chili butter. Remove them and deglaze the pan with about 3 ½ tbsp. of the cooking stock. Reduce until thickened and rectify the taste with a dash of lemon juice.

**THE ONIONS**

Sauté the thinly sliced onion hearts in very hot oil for about 7-8 minutes. Drain on kitchen paper.

**PRESENTATION**

With the cardoon pieces, form a 10cm (4 in) square in an oven dish, and repeat the process in four layers, changing the angle for each layer. Drizzle with the reduced cooking jus and finish with the Parmesan shavings. Grill for about 10 minutes. To serve, place the cardoons on hot plates and garnish with the butter curls, parsley leaves and sautéed onions.

# Quail roasted in lemon ginger butter

Preparation time
**10 minutes**

Cooking time
**10 minutes**

**Serves 4**

10 g (¼ oz) fresh ginger

1 organic lemon

100 g (⅔ cup) semi-salted butter

100 g (3 oz) Red Meat radishes

1 swede (rutabaga)

150 g (4 ½ oz) helianthis (or jerusalem artichokes)

16 grey shallots

1 lid seal (mix 2 cups flour with 15cl
(½ cup) water to form a paste)

4 dressed quails weighing 160g (4-5 oz) each

50 cl (2 cups) chicken stock

100 g (1 cup) cress

Oil

**PREPARATION**

The day before, grate the ginger and lemon zest and using a fork, combine them with the softened salted butter. Cover with cling film and chill the flavoured butter.

**THE VEGETABLES**

Next day, sauté the radishes and quartered swede with the remaining butter in a covered pan. Slice the helianthis or jerusalem artichokes thinly with a mandolin and fry in the oil at 160°C (320°F). Rub the unpeeled shallots with oil, salt them and place in a lidded cast-iron pot, sealing the lid with the flour paste. Bake for 20 minutes at 180°C (360°F).

**THE QUAILS**

Roast the quails in part of the infused butter, turning onto the sides to protect the breasts that should be siezed over a gentle heat after 20 minutes. Leave in a warm oven (100°C, 212°F, th 3-4) in another dish. Meanwhile, make a jus in the cast iron pot by whipping the cooking butter into the chicken stock.

**PRESENTATION**

Present the boned quails on hot plates surrounded by the vegetables, garnishing with the jerusalem artichoke chips, cress and jus.

# New potatoes, purple carrots and vanilla butter

Preparation time
**45 minutes**

Cooking time
**30 minutes**

**Serves 4**

200 g (1 ⅓ cup) vanilla butter

2 purple carrots

10 cl (½ cup) chicken stock

400 g (15 oz) new charlotte potatoes (about 40)

4 spring onions

60 g (2 ½ oz) samphire

Sunflower oil

Salt

**PREPARATION**

Take a large flat plate, cover it with a tightly stretched cling film. and place in the freezer. Using a peeling knive, take 40 curls of vanilla butter and place on the filmed plate (if the butter softens too quickly, return to the freezer and continue the operation). Keep the plate in the freezer.

**THE CARROTS**

Peel the carrots (leave aside the peel) and then, using a mandolin, cut 40 very thin identical slices lengthwise,. Fry them in the sunflower oil at 140° C (284°F) for about six minutes (the carrot chips must be dry but not too dark) then drain on kitchen paper. Cut up the carrot peel and boil in a saucepan with the chicken stock until cooked. Drain off the stock, set it aside and smoothly purée the carrots with a mixer.

**THE NEW POTATOES**

In a covered cast iron pot, fry the cleaned potatoes in their skins in the remaining vanilla butter for ten minutes, shaking gently and regularly, making sure the butter does not brown too much, then add the sliced onions. Salt and cook gently (about 20 minutes), regularly taking off the lid to let off steam and keep a residue of frothy butter.

**PRESENTATION**

Once cooked, present each potato on a teaspoonful of onion confit, and place dots of carrot purée between the potatoes. Top each with a carrot chip and sprinkle with samphire. Make a jus by deglazing the potato butter with the stock from the carrots. Add a dash of jus to each plate and a curl of butter on each potato.

Tip: to cover anything with butter, the filmed plate in the freezer is a good way to prepare a butter "skin" easy to unstick with a spatula. The fresh butter taste is thus kept intact.

# Roasted veal cutlets
# in a tajine pot

Preparation time
**1 hour**

Cooking time
**45 minutes**

**Serves 4**

2 large (300g or ½ lb) veal cutlets

250 g (1 ⅔ cups) tajine butter

200 g (7 oz) grey shallots

1 garlic clove

10 cl (½ cup) chicken stock

500 gr (1 lb) endives or mesclun

Olive oil

Cider vinegar

### PREPARATION

Leave the meat at room temperature for 1 hour beforehand.

In a large cast iron pot, heat 150g (1 cup) tajine butter over a very low flame with the peeled shallots and unpeeled garlic, until it begins to froth.

### THE VEAL CUTLETS

Brown the veal cutlets on both sides in this fat, then stand them vertically and baste constantly with the butter using a spoon. Add about 30g (¼ cup) each time you baste, to prevent the cooking butter separating and beginning to burn. Cooking in the pot can take about 45 minutes, since the meat must be turned constantly and the heat of the butter checked so that it does not burn while still searing the cutlets (if you opt to bake the meat at 180°C (360°F) instead, it takes half as long).

Once cooked, place the meat on a hot plate to rest and finish the jus by deglazing the pot with the chicken stock. Reduce and whip in the butter.

### PRESENTATION

Carve the cutlets and present on hot plates, accompanied by a salad of endives or mesclun seasoned with cider vinegar and olive oil.

# Clarified butter and parsley French fries

Preparation time
**40 minutes**

Cooking time
**30 minutes**

**Serves 4**

2 kg (4 ½ lb) semi-salted butter

1 bunch parsley

1 kg (2 lb) firm waxy potatoes (eg. Charlotte)

Sunflower oil

**THE CLARIFIED BUTTER**

Bring the water in the bottom of the double saucepan to the boil; the butter will gradually decant into three parts: the protein part (the froth) on the top, the clarified butter below and the whey part at the bottom. To separate them and collect the clarified butter, first completely remove the froth with a spoon and then pour the clarified butter into a saucepan, stopping just before getting to the whey.

Fry the parsley in the clarified butter at 140°C (285°F) then drain it on kitchen paper and salt it.

**THE POTATOES**

Peel the potatoes and cut into fingers. Then pre-fry them in the clarified butter at 150°C (300°F) for about 7 minutes. This is called « blanching » them.

**PRESENTATION**

Just before serving, fry the french fries again at 175°C (350°F) just long enough to brown them and make them crisp. Drain, then salt them and garnsh with the fried parsley.

# Chocolate tart, sabayon and tonka bean butter

**Make 12 hr ahead**

Preparation time
**45 minutes**

Cooking time
**20 minutes**

Serves 4

For the chocolate sugar crust pastry:

130 g (nearly 1 cup) semi-salted butter

1 grated tonka bean

120 g (1 cup) confectioner's sugar

180 g (1 ⅓ cups) all-purpose flour

1 egg

40 g (½ cup) cocoa powder

For the sabayon:

4 egg yolks

75 g (¾ cup) confectioner's sugar

8 tbsp water

24 dark chocolate coins

**THE CHOCOLATE SUGARCRUST PASTRY**

The day before, beat together the butter and the grated tonka bean. Chill overnight.

The next day, preheat the oven to 180°C (360°F, th. 6). Using a flat beater, mix together the sugar, the flavoured butter cut into small cubes, the flour, the cocoa powder and the egg. Roll out the dough to a thickness of ⅛ inch between two sheets of greaseproof paper. Cut out four discs 12 cm (5 in) in diameter and line four 4-inch tartlet tins . Bake at 180°C (360°F) for 15 minutes.

**THE SABAYON**

In a small double saucepan, whip the egg yolks with the sugar and the water. The sabayon should not be too runny.

**PRESENTATION**

Pour the sabayon into the tartlet shells, then top with the chocolate coins. Heat under the grill until the sabayon is slightly browned.

# Butternut Tatin with curry butter

Preparation time
**20 minutes**

Cooking time
**55 minutes**

**Serves 4**

For the sugarcrust pastry:

100 g (⅔ cup) semi-salted butter

100 g (1 cup) confectioner's sugar

180 g (1 ⅓ cups) flour

3 egg yolks

For the butternut with curry butter:

50 g (⅓ cup) curry butter

25 g (¼ cup) confectioner's sugar

500 g (3 ¾ cups) butternut squash

1 organic lime

**THE SUGAR CRUST TATIN PASTRY**

Preheat the oven to 180°C (360°F, th. 6). With a flat beater, mix the butter, sugar and flour together. When everything is mixed, add the yolks to form a dough. Roll this out to a thickness of ¼ in between two greaseproof paper sheets. Cut out four circles of pastry to the size of the tartlet tins and bake at 180°C (360°F) for 17 minutes.

**THE BUTTERNUT WITH CURRY BUTTER**

Preheat the oven to 150°C (300°F). Mix the curry butter with the sugar, spread it flat and cut out 4 discs the size of the tartlets. Place them between two layers of cling film and chill.

Cut the butternut into cubes, place them in the tartlet tins and cover them with the curry butter discs. Bake for 30 – 35 minutes at 150°C (300°F).

**PRESENTATION**

To serve, turn out the caramelized butternut confit onto the shortbreads, and top with grated lime zest.

Serve warm.

# Baked apples, Sichuan pepper butter and nuts

Preparation time
**15 minutes**

Cooking time
**1 ½ hours**

**Serves 4**

5 red, sharp flavoured apples (eg rubinette)

50 g (⅓ cup) whole hazelnuts

50 g (⅓ cup) whole almonds

70 g (⅔ cup) sugar

100 g (⅔ cup) Sichuan pepper butter

1 organic orange

**PREPARATION**

Core the apples and place in an oven dish. Block the hole at the bottom of each apple with a hazelnut and an almond so that the butter will stay inside the apple while cooking and gently confit it.

**SICHUAN BUTTER AND NUTS**

Mash the butter and sugar to a smooth mix. Roughly crush the rest of the almonds and hazelnuts and add them to the mixture, then grate the orange zest over it.

Preheat the oven to 130°C (270°F, th. 4-5). Fill the holes in the apples with the flavoured butter and bake for 1 ½ hours at 130°C (270°F).

After removing from the oven, deglaze the caramel with a little orange juice and baste it generously over the apples. Serve warm.

# Roasted pineapple,
# curry butter caramel

Preparation time
**30 minutes**

Cooking time
**1 hour**

**Serves 4**

1 Reunion Island Victoria pineapple
(or equivalent strongly flavoured small pineapple)

200 g (2 cups) confectioner's sugar

15 cl (½ cup) water

100 g (⅔ cup) curry butter

1 organic lime

**THE PINEAPPLE**

Peel the pineapple with a sawtoothed knife, keeping the leaves. Wrap the leaves in greaseproof paper tied with kitchen string so that they do not burn during cooking.

Preheat the oven to 140°C (285°F, th. 4-5).

**THE CURRY BUTTER CARAMEL**

Make a caramel from the sugar and 5 cl (3 ½ tbsp) water heated to 160°C (320°F), then take the pan off the flame and uncook it as follows: gradually pour in the remaining water to stop the cooking (warning: this should be done carefully as the steam generated, or a splash of the caramel, can burn). Then whip the curry butter into the warm caramel.

**PRESENTATION**

Place the pineapple in an oven dish, pour over the curry caramel and bake for about 1 hour at 140°C (285°F). Turn and baste the pineapple constantly.

When ready to serve, sprinkle the whole pineapple with grated lime zest and rectify the taste of the syup with the lime juice.

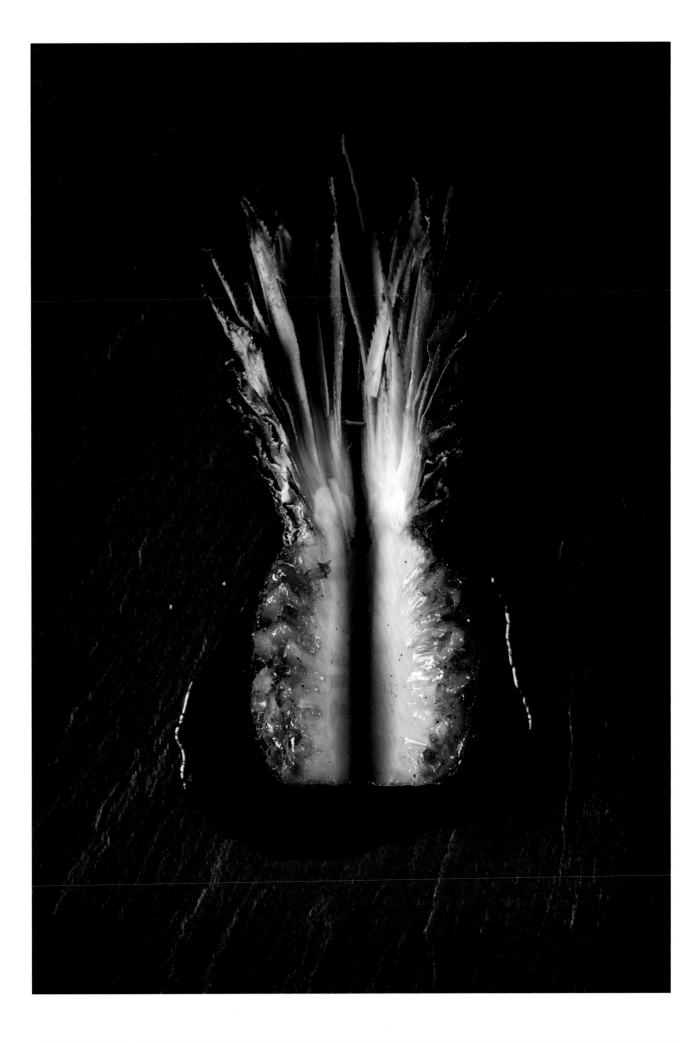

# Salted butter
# caramel crunchers

Preparation time
**30 minutes**

Cooking time
**30 minutes**

**Serves 4**

For the salted butter caramel ice cream:

15 cl (½ cup) single cream

200 g (1 ⅓ cups) semi-salted butter

250 g (2 ½ cups) confectioner's sugar

1 l (4 cups) milk

For the crunchy cookies:

200 g (2 cups) baker's sugar

100 g (¾ cup) all-purpose flour

60 g egg whites (= 2 egg whites)

100 g (⅔ cup) unsalted butter, melted

**THE SALTED BUTTER CARAMEL ICE CREAM**

In a saucepan over a hot flame, mix the cream, butter and sugar and heat to 170°C (340°F), giving a nice dark caramel. Stop the cooking by gradually pouring in the milk, off the heat, to avoid being burned by the steam or the caramel splashes. Bring to the boil to melt all the caramel, leave to cool and then churn in an ice cream maker.

**THE CRUNCHY COOKIES**

Preheat the oven to 180°C (360°F, th. 6). Combine all the ingredients to form a smooth dough. Spread this dough thinly using a right-angle spatula to press it onto a non stick surface and make 10 cm (4 in) squares.
Bake at 180°C (360°F) for 15 minutes.

**PRESENTATION**

Present the crunchy cookies on plates, alternating ice cream and cookies. They can be served accompanied by chocolate sauce.

# Breton shortbread, lemon and yuzu butter cream

Preparation time
**45 minutes**

Cooking time
**30 minutes**

**Serves 4**

For the lemon/yuzu cream:

20 cl (¾ cup) lemon juice

5 g (1 rounded tsp) powdered gelatin

6 eggs

100 g (1 cup) confectioner's sugar

175 g (1 ⅕ cup) yuzu butter

For the Breton shortbread:

120 g (¾ cup) semi-salted butter

120 g (1 ¼ cups) confectioner's sugar

180 g (1 ⅓ cup) all-purpose flour

7 g (1 ½ tsp) baking soda

3 egg yolks (60 g, 2 oz)

50 gr (1 ½ oz) meringues

### THE LEMON/YUZU CREAM

Boil the lemon juice in a saucepan with the gelatin. In a round metal mixing bowl, beat the eggs with the sugar until creamy, then add the boiled lemon mixture. Return the mixture to the lemon juice saucepan and heat for 3-4 minutes, whipping vigorously. Pour the resulting cream back into the round mixing bowl and leave to cool. Once tepid, add in the yuzu butter cut into small cubes. Chill for about 4 hours.

### THE BRETON SHORTBREAD

Mix the butter cut into small cubes, the sugar, the flour and the baking soda together with a flat beater. Once they are well mixed, beat in the egg yolks. Roll out this dough between two greaseproof paper sheets to a thickness of 1 cm (¼ in) and chill for one hour. After that, preheat the oven to 180°C (360°F, th. 6), cut the dough into four 10cm (4-in) squares, and cut each square in half diagonally. Bake for 20 minutes at 180°C (360°F).

### PRESENTATION

When the shortbread triangles are cold and ready to serve, beat the cream with a food mixer for 3-4 minutes and place it in a pastry bag with a plain nozzle. Present the shortbreads topped with small dots of cream and garnished with meringue sticks.

# Buckwheat cracker and chocolate cream

Preparation time
**40 minutes**

Cooking time
**20 minutes**

**Serves 4**

For the buckwheat cracker:

30 cl (1 ¼ cups) water

300 g (1 ⅔ cups) sesame flour

210 g (1 ½ cups) semi-salted butter

30 g (¼ cup) sugar

1 egg white (30 g, nearly 1 oz)

For the chocolate cream:

85 cl (3 ½ cups) liquid cream

85 cl (3 ½ cups) milk

2 egg yolks (40g, 1 oz)

25 g confectioner's sugar

110 g (⅔ cup) dark chocolate

**THE BUCKWHEAT CRACKER**

Preheat the oven to 160°C (320°F, th. 5-6). Boil the water and pour in the buckwheat flour. Mix well with a spatula and while still warm, add the butter cut into cubes and the sugar. Finally, when the mixture is cold, mix in the egg white. Spread the dough thinly on a non-stick tray using a spatula, to form 20 identical 12 cm (5 in) rectangles, then bake at 160°C (320°F) for 15 minutes.

**THE CHOCOLATE CREAM**

For the custard: boil the cream and milk together, pour them onto the yolks previously mixed with the sugar, and then cook (without bringing to the boil) for 2 minutes over a low flame. Melt the chocolate and pour in the custard, beating the mixture with a hand beater to make it smooth. Cover with cling film and chill.

**PRESENTATION**

Using a pastry bag, garnish the buckwheat crackers with the cream and pile them up into a mille feuille.

# GLOSSARY

**AMF**: anhydrous milk fat is used in industrial production. It must contain at least 99.8% milk fat and is made from milk, using a process that eliminates virtually all of the water and non-fat solids.

**AOP**: Appellation d'Origine Protégée is an EU-wide system of protection following on from the French AOC system. There are three AOP French butters: AOP Beurre Charentes-Poitou, AOP Beurre d'Isigny and AOP Beurre de Bresse (respectively awarded an AOC in 1979, 1986 and 2012.)

***Basset***: a type of French woven basket used to contain 5-10kg (11-22lb) of butter.

***Beurrerie***: a butter workshop, dairy, equipped with all the facilities required to transform milk into butter. The concept of the beurrerie dates from the late 19th century, in contrast to the batch production traditionally associated with butter-making.

**Brittle**: describes the texture of butter in winter.

**Butter**: a product exclusively produced by churning cream (ie milk or its by-products), from which sufficient milk and water has been removed by kneading and washing to leave no more than 18g (0.63oz) of non-fat material per 100g (4oz), of which no more than 16g water (0.56oz). Butter is a water-and-oil emulsion.

**Butter consumption**: The French eat eight kilograms (17.6lb) of butter per person per year, making them the world's biggest per-capita consumers of butter.

**Butter knife**: 16th century utensil made of pear, box or beech wood, used to cut butter. Butter knives forming part of a tableware set are distinguished by a rounded end.

**Buttermilk**: the milky liquid extracted in the course of churning the milk or cream. Its composition depends on the fatty acids in the cream and the characteristics of the water used to wash the butter grains.

**Butter mold**: 18th century utensil made of pear, box or beech wood,, for shaping butter into original geometric shapes and imprinting a low relief design that left an impression on top when the butter was released from the mold. Butter molds consisted of three movable sections: a carved lid and two hinged sides that opened to release the butter. Their invention marked a milestone for the butter industry, as the first example of mechanization and as a way to identify the provenance of the butter. The forerunner of the label, so to speak.

**Butter oil**: a technical butter made from milk fat (AMF) in liquid form, used in breads, cakes and pastries.

**Butter paddle**: 16th century utensil in pear-wood, boxwood or beech wood, with a smooth or grooved surface, used to shape butter at the point of sale.

**Butter stamp**: an 18th century tool made of pear, box or beech wood for stamping the maker's mark into butter. Cows, flowers, birds and coats of arms were among the most decorative butter stamps.

**Calico**: a rather coarse-woven cotton, once used as a fabric wrapping for 25kg of butter (55lb).

***Cassant***: French term meaning "brittle" used to describe the texture of butter in winter.

**Centrifugal separation**: the mechanical process that separates the components of a mixture according to density. Its invention revolutionized the dairy industry and served as the basis for the centrifugal separator manufactured by Gustaf de Laval in 1878, which is still widely used today. Centrifugal separation makes it possible to separate cream from milk faster and more efficiently than ever before – a determining factor in the butter-making process.

**Churn**: a device used to shake milk or cream to make butter. The churn is filled half full and driven by a motor that rotates the drum around a fixed axis. Churns come in all shapes (barrel-shaped, box-shaped, cone-shaped) and are typically made of wood, aluminum or stainless steel.

**Churned butter**: it took until 13 July 1993 for the Appeal Court in Rennes to rule that the words *beurre de baratte* (churned butter) can only apply to butter that is exclusively produced by churning. It cannot apply to butter that is made in a continuous butter making machine, even if the final kneading takes place in a churn. Before then, the butter industry was pretty unscrupulous about labeling. There was nothing to prevent butter made in a butter-making machine from being labeled *beurre de baratte* or featuring a drawing of a churn on the packaging.

**Churning**: the process of shaking up cream to make butter in a churn, using liquid cream at a temperature of 13-14°C (55-57°F) depending on the season. The process is divided into three stages. Stage One: the cream changes from liquid to solid (known as "phase inversion") causing the fat globules to rise to the surface where they form a foamy mass of fat particles called the "butter grains". Stage Two: the door of the churn is opened to reveal these yellow grains floating at the top of a pale whitish liquid – the buttermilk, which is drawn off through a drain outlet at the bottom of the churn. All that remains in the churn are the butter grains, which must now be washed to remove any residual butterfat. This involves adding a quantity of iced water to the butterfat then moving the churn forward and backward until washing is complete. This rinsing water is then likewise drained off and replaced with a volume of iced water equivalent to the quantity of buttermilk removed at the end of the first stage. Stage Three: the contents are churned again to make a water-in-oil emulsion. The difference in temperature between the cream at 13-14°C (55-57°F – see above) and the iced water causes the butter grains to contract and agglomerate as the churn is rotated, producing that noble material, butter. Churning is a discontinuous process that works the butter to a continuous fat phase.

**Color**: the color of butter depends on what the cows eat. In spring and summer they graze on juicy, green grass that produces chlorophyll (the pigment that makes grass green) and beta-keratin (the red-orange pigment that gives butter its color). The color of butter also varies with the season: buttercup yellow in the growing season (spring and summer) verging on pale yellow to white with ivory reflections in the forage season (autumn and winter). Other typical colors are cream and pale or bright gold with glossy, sometimes shiny reflections. But this applies only to handmade butters. Industrial butters undergo no such change. They remain the same color all year round, as required by marketing experts. Nor do they present any of those variations and irregularities seen with artisan butters. Those tear-like drops of water that well up to the top of grass-fed butters are unacceptable in the butter industry because they make the color uneven (they also fall foul of competition rules).

**Concentrated butter**: a technical butter made from anhydrous milk fat (AMF) in solid form, with a higher fat content that ordinary butter. Used in breads, cakes and pastries.

**Continuous butter-making machine**: a machine that allows for the continuous production of butter. Designed for large-scale production and optimal performance, but it significantly alters the nature of cream, delivering butter of very indifferent quality.

*Coulée*: literally "flow", meaning the mass of finished butter that flows out of the churn at the end of the operation.

**Cream**: fat-rich milk. The cream separates because milk fat is lower in density (lighter) than skimmed milk. This will occur spontaneously in milk that is left to stand or subjected to a centrifugal force.

**Creaming**: the spontaneous separation of the fat globules, which rise to the top of milk that is left to stand – the traditional method of creaming before the invention of the centrifugal creamer.

*Délaitage*: literally "de-milking" – the removal of the buttermilk from the churn.

*Demi-beurre*: outmoded term for low-fat or light butters.

*Demie de beurre*: French name for a 250g (one pound) pack of butter.

**Extra-fine butter**: made exclusively from fresh, pasteurized cream that has never been frozen or deep-frozen. Manufacturing must commence within 72 hours of milk or cream collection, churning within 48 hours of skimming.

**Fine butter**: made from pasteurized cream that contains no more than 30 percent of frozen or deep-frozen raw ingredients.

**Flavored butters**: an invention that originated with French housewives, peasants and the nobility. In the 17th century, the Marquise de Sévigné and Madame Fouquet penned recipes for butters blended with fresh herbs and flowers, used for cooking and therapeutic purposes. Madame de Sévigné writes in her letters to her daughter the Countess de Grignan that she loves biting into fresh Brittany butter, that her son "left his teeth marks in the butter" and that she sprinkles it with "fresh herbs and violets." Recipes to make your mouth water! Madame Fouquet was meanwhile the author of *The Remedies of Madame Fouquet*, one of the most famous collections of popular remedies.

**Flavor**: a term encompassing taste, aroma and mouth-feel.

*Goûte-beurre*: literally "a butter taster" – a small boxwood knife with a beveled end dating from the 19th century.

**Home butter churn**: a small churn, usually made of glass and equipped with a wooden agitator, used for making butter at home. In the late 18th century, some were engraved with the crest of the chateau that held sway over the farm producing the butter. More recently, in the 20th century, the French company Perlor became famous for its home butter churns.

# GLOSSARY

**Kneader**: originally the person who worked the butter by hand, removing the buttermilk, adding the salt. Then in the late 19th century (c. 1875-1880), the Etablissements Simon in Cherbourg developed a rotary kneader with teak table.

**Kneading**: this may be a mechanical or a manual process. A kneading machine pulverizes the fat globules in the aqueous phase, causing the butter grains to clump together. This is how industrial butters are kneaded. A kneading table works to soften the texture of butter and make it more elastic. This method also keeps the butter in contact with the air, oxygenating the fat content and bringing complexity to the bouquet. Bordier Butter is always kneaded in this fashion.

**Low-fat butter**: pseudo-butter with a lower milk-fat content than real butter (39-41% compared to 60-62%). Products in this category must be labeled *spécialité laitière à tartiner à x %* (dairy spread containing xxx % fat). Products in this "category" are a record-breaking cocktail of emulsifiers, preservatives, acidity regulators, flavorings and thickeners. For pity's sake, watch out for yourselves and your family! The only benefit of these butters is "public health discourse" – that and a liberal smattering of vitamins (A, D and E) that goes down well with health professionals. But they are in fact a gigantic conjuring trick, made by people who think they know better than Nature. People who have forgotten that old saying "all things in moderation and moderation in all things." But then good sense has never been a money-spinner …

**Milk**: as defined in France in 1909, milk for human consumption is "the whole, unmodified product of the complete and uninterrupted milking of a healthy, well-nourished dairy cow that is not over-milked. It should be collected under hygienic conditions and contain no colostrum."

**Moisture content**: the quantity of water in butter, as measured by analysis, which must be not less than 12 percent. This includes relative moisture such as those droplets of water that well up to the top when Jean-Yves Bordier works his butter on the kneading table. This is visible moisture, particularly noticeable after salting, not a sign of high total moisture content.

**Motte or moche**: tall mounds of butter weighing 1-10kg (2-22lb). The *motte* is part of the history of French butter.

**Muslin**: a very fine, gauze-like fabric used to wrap mounds of butter until the 1980s, particularly in the Isigny-sur-Mer region of Normandy.

**Organic butter**: butter made from organic cream, as defined by specific rules focused on aspects such as respect for the environment and animal welfare. In France the AB label is used to identify products that meet organic certification requirements. It distinguishes a commendable approach to the production of the raw material for butter – but it offers no guarantees as to the quality of the process involved in transforming milk to butter. So an organic butter may well have been made in a continuous butter-making machine, in which case "organic" does not necessarily mean "good"!

**Oxidation**: the process that brings out the complex flavors in butter.

**Pain Milan**: flat-topped, vertical, slightly trapezoidal *mottes* of butter, once widely produced in the Deux-Sèvres region (central west France).

**Parchment paper**: a 20th century invention, widely known in France as *papier à beurre*. It replaced the sorrel or cabbage leaves that were previously used by farmers' wives to transport then sell their butter at the market. Parchment paper marked a breakthrough because it allowed producers to label their butters – add their signature, name, address and design of their choosing. Technically speaking, kitchen parchment is paper that has been treated with sulfuric acid to close up the pores between the fibers. The result is a greaseproof and waterproof paper that is widely used in the bread, cake and pastry industry for its heat-resistant properties. The dairy industry prefers to use aluminum foil, which is a great shame because parchment paper poses none of the health risks associated with aluminum foil. The potential dangers of aluminum in food are still being hotly debated by scientists.

**Pasteurized butter**: made from heat-treated cream, which gives butter a much longer shelf life than its raw counterpart and preserves it flavors.

**Quart de beurre**: French term for a 125g (4.4oz) pack of butter.

**Raw butter**: made from cream that has not been heat-treated. Raw butter has a shorter shelf life than pasteurized butter and can rapidly develop off-flavors and turn rancid.

**Shelf life**: Bordier Butter will keep for three weeks in the refrigerator at 0-6°C (32-43°F), rising to 12 months when stored in the freezer. For best results, keep the butter in its original packaging, wrapped in aluminum foil to block out UV rays.

**Spreadability**: butter is best kept in the fridge, for health reasons and to avoid those rancid tastes that come with premature aging. The 1970s then saw the launch of margarines that were "spreadable straight from the fridge." So the butter industry, determined not to lag behind in technology, developed a technique for making soft butters that were spreadable "straight from the fridge". This required the splitting of the oleic acids so as to separate out the

fatty acids that make up butter fat. What you then have is a mix of soft and normal butter. In the early 20th century, New Zealand butter-makers already had the idea of kneading the morning's churning with the evening's churning so as to produce a butter that remained soft at all times.

**Taste**: the flavor profile of the butter, depending on the season, the cows and the dairy farmer. The season, because it has an influence on the characteristics and nutritional properties of pastureland. The cows, because they produce the milk that goes into butter, some breeds of cow being better at this than others. The dairy farmers because, in addition to everything else, they look out for the welfare of the animals: milking them gently, trying alternative remedies before resorting to antibiotics, and feeding them properly. That means good pasture composed of clover, alfalfa, flowers and other plants typical of the terroir. Not to mention good quality hay, grown and dried on the farm in a large hay dryer. All of these factors contribute to the taste profile of butter. Any off-flavors will in any case by detected by manufacturing quality control and the butter in question will be withdrawn. Examples of flavor taints range from sharp, bitter, overly salty or overpowering flavors to major flaws such as a rancid, cheesy or oxidized taste; rank flavors of silage, boiled milk and cream that is past its best; and a whiff of sourness, "cow's breath" or other "barnyard" flavors.

**Udder**: an organ formed of the mammary glands of domestic mammals. It is composed of two pairs of glands, each with a finger-shaped teat that squirts out milk when squeezed. The udder is part of the mammary reservoir. Its vascular system carries blood to the reservoir via a network of arteries, pumping blood at the rate of 300 liters of blood for every one liter of milk produced!

# ADRESSES

**For bread lovers**

Henrik Robino in St. Malo,
Jean-Paul Vezziano in Antibes,
Jean-Luc Poujauran, Apollonia Poilâne
and Thierry Breton in Paris!

My favorite bakeries!

**For wine lovers**

Yannick Heude, la Cave de l'Abbaye
Saint-Jean, in St. Malo old town.

Jean-Pierre Lécluze, le Cellier
Saint-Germain, in Rennes.

Don't miss *Les Vins de Ma Vie* by Eric
Beaumard (Editions de La Martinière.)

**For fish and shellfish lovers**

Fishmonger Gilles Guinemer, in St. Malo
old town.

Jean-Yves Bourcier, owner-fisherman in
Lancieux.

**For oysters lovers**

Maison Pichot, La Tsarskaya, in Cancale.

**For meat lovers**

Boucherie Charcuterie Traiteur Olivier
Ruellan, in St. Malo – high quality meat,
charcuterie and deli-fare.

**For fruit and vegetable lovers**

Mickaël Robin, a market gardener from
Saint-Méloir-des-Ondes, selling at the
Paramé market in St. Malo.

Juliette and Estelle at Les 4 Saisons in
St. Malo old town.

**For patisserie lovers**

Try the *kouign-amann* at
La Maison du Pain, in St. Malo old town.

Also the rum babas from Pierre Rousseaux
and Luc Mobihan in St. Malo old town
(Les Babas de Saint-Malo).

**For food lovers**

Le Saint-Placide, in St. Servan (St. Malo)
for Isabelle and Luc Mobihan's delicious
cooking and good wines, amply worthy
of Michelin recognition.

Le Bénétin, where chef Arnaud Beruel
works wonders with his favorite produce.
Fine sea view. St. Malo Rothéneuf.

Breizh Café Bertrand Larcher and La
Crêpe Autrement, in St. Malo old town.

The Lion d'Or and the Café de l'Ouest,
run by brothers Thibault and Morgan
Hector, in St. Malo old town.

Le Zag, run by Sylvaine and Olivier.
Excellent pizza by the water in Dinan.

Auberge du Pont d'Acigné,
Sylvain Guillemot, Pré d'Acigné,
35530 Noyal-sur-Vilaine

**For cake lovers**

Pâtisserie Stéphane Denis, in St. Servan
(St. Malo). Understated excellence!

**For coffee lovers**

Mokamalo in St. Malo old town

# ACKNOWLEDGEMENTS

My thanks to Géraldine Péan and Aurélie Rousseaux, for their able management of Bordier Butter! For their good-natured running of the business, their skills and everything else. From the bottom of my heart, I thank all those team members who share our undivided commitment to the pursuit of excellence.
My sincere thanks to each and every one of you!

My respect and gratitude go to Raymond Garnier and Christian Guignard. Without your input dear Raymond – your unfailing availability, active listening and expertise – Bordier Butter would not be the success it is today. Christian, you taught me the art of analysis – how to keep a cool head and respond appropriately to any situation. Together the two of you gave Bordier Butter the tools it needed to meet modern standards of health and safety, without compromising those traditional values that are the key to its excellence.
My heartfelt thanks to you both.

No book is ever long enough to mention everyone – dear friends like Monsieur Poujauran, Monsieur Celbert, Jean-Luc and Jean-Francois, to mention but a few. Thank you, my fellow bread-breakers, my *co-pains*, for your precious friendship.

Thanks to all you Brittany chefs past and present for your vote of confidence. Thanks to my great friend Monsieur Jacques Guillo and Madame Gestin in Ploumanac'h who were my first customers in 1982. Thanks also to the Tirel family and Jean-Pierre Crouzil in Plancoët, to Michel Saint-Cast and Olivier in Cancale, and so many others too. Words cannot express how grateful I am to you all. True friendship never fades!

Heartfelt thanks to those Brittany catering colleges that defend and promote craft practices! The schools of La Guerche, in Saint-Méen-le-Grand, and Dinard deserve particular mention. Thanks to Éliane Autun and Patrick Hamard, also Alain Bernard, Claude Mayol, Jean-Baptiste Gailly and all of the teaching staff for their dedication and first-rate teaching!

A big thank-you to Roland Beaumanoir and Yves Fantou, the gifted founders of La Place Gourmande.

Thanks to you Monsieur Jean, and you Florence, and you too, Geneviève, for your efficiency in the shadow of giants!

Thanks to my town St. Malo for watching me grow.

And thanks above all to all of my customers, without whom Bordier Butter would not exist!

Graphic design and art work: Justeciel
Translation from French to English: Florence Brutton
Proofreading: Mark Brutton

Translation of recipes : Gabrielle Smart-Fouquet
Photoengraving: Point 11
ISBN: 978-1- 4197-3847-0

**ABRAMS**
The Art of Books

195 Broadway
New York, NY 10007
Abramsbooks.com